Sangha Speaks

Mark Griffin

Sangha Speaks

Stories,
Poems and Artwork
by
Hard Light Sangha Members

Hard Light Publishing
23852 Pacific Coast Highway, Suite 488
Malibu, CA 90265
Website: www.hardlight.org
© 2007 by Hard Light Publishing
All rights reserved. Published 2007

ISBN 978-0-9759020-1-1

Editor: Pat Cookinham
Associate Editor: Doug Ertman
Cover Design: Vanig Torikian
Cover Photograph: Getty Images
Interior Design: Vanig Torikian
Production: V. LeRossignol Blades

All rights reserved. This book may not be reproduced in whole or in part or transmitted in any form, or by any means electronic, mechanical, photocopying, recording, or other, without written permission from the publisher, except by a reviewer who may quote brief passages in a review.

Library of Congress Cataloging - in – Publication Data
    Hard Light Sangha
    Sangha Speaks/Hard Light Sangha
      p. cm.
    ISBN: 978-0-9759020-1-1 (alk. paper)
1. Spiritual Life. I. Title: Sangha speaks.

Selfless service is the fastest way to Enlightenment!

—Mark Griffin

contents

xi   Foreword, *Mark Griffin*
xiii Introduction, *Doug Ertman*

The Search

3   through the looking glass, *Lauren Freiman*
4   Searching for God in Los Angeles, *Lauri Fraser*
6   Truth, *Johanne Joseph*
7   Steps to Liberation, *Nadia Marie Harding*
10 A Mystery, *Anonymous*
11 Listening, *Wanda Rhodes*
12 Pursuit, *Bob Schulenburg*

The Guru

14 Letter to the Guru, *Dr. Shanta Shirset*
15 Meeting the Guru, *Ann Brockway*
16 My Teacher—Guru Mark, *Astrid Cheney*
18 Reflections of Self, *Wanda Rhodes*
19 The Mystery of Shaktipat, *Bart Walton*
22 The Good Shepherd, *Tunga Nath (Matt Hodges)*
26 Bless the charming gardener, *Jason Handler*
27 The Three Blessings of the Guru, *Jeffrey Evan Stamm*
30 The Holy Ruby Mine, *Eva Stattine*
33 The Tale of the Mouse, *Jeffrey Evan Stamm*
36 I Breathe for My Guru, *Tim Maloney*
45 Teh Teh La La, *Nathan Goreham*

The Sangha

48 Dear Reader, *Eliana R. Farias*
50 The Hard Light Way, *Pauline Arneberg*
52 Hard Light: Modern Life Meets Timeless Truth, *Doug Allen*
54 Studying with Mark, *Judith Bluestone Polich*
56 Light, Love, and Emptiness, *Fernando Escobar*
59 Don't Come—You Wouldn't Like It, *Bob Schulenburg*
61 Thank You, *Mandy Hooper*

contents

The Practice
- 64 My Sitting Meditation, *Anonymous*
- 65 Sangha Populus Tremuloides, *Barbara Jo Fleming*
- 67 Rising Sun, *Barbara Hogan*
- 68 crashcourse, *Virginia LeRossignol Blades*
- 73 Sitting still, *Jason Handler*
- 74 Rising Sun: Spiritual Masters and the Art of Meditation, *Alyson Dutch*
- 80 Electronic Conversations, *Bob Schulenburg*
- 83 Meditation Intensive, *Kai Markowitz*
- 87 Totems, *Brian Hughes*
- 88 Empty Vessel, *Wanda Rhodes*

The Experience
- 90 The Lemmings, *Rudrakshananda*
- 91 Gracewaves, *Paige Hetherington*
- 93 The names i'll call her, *Jason Handler*
- 94 Old Song, *Linda Horan*
- 95 The Tale of the Siddha, *Bob Schulenburg*
- 97 The moment we touched, *Jason Handler*
- 98 Emptiness, Wrathful Annihilation of Identity, *Siddha Student*
- 99 The Five Phases, *Anonymous*
- 100 THAT'S NOT MINE!, *Camille Harris*
- 102 Where everything connects, *Jason Handler*
- 103 Progression, *Pat Cookinham*
- 104 Awakening, *Rachel Leach*
- 106 Two Haiku, *Wanda Rhodes*

The Ladder
- 109 Burning Man, *Bob Schulenburg*
- 110 The Ladder, *Lauren Freiman*
- 113 Ladder 108, *Paige Hetherington*
- 114 So'ham City, *Fernando Escobar*
- 117 Climbing the Ladder, *Tim Maloney*

contents

The Dark Voyage

- 121 Direct Report, *Hal Barkhouse*
- 122 How Will I Ever Survive INDIA?, *Lauri Fraser*
- 124 Fear and Loathing in India, *Brian Stephens*
- 127 India 2003, *Marcelle Marshall*
- 128 into the ganga, *Lauren Freiman*
- 130 Pictures of India, *Mandy Hooper*
- 133 Second Time Around, *Jan Myers*
- 134 Oh, What's so Great about India?, *Hal Barkhouse*
- 135 India Yatra 2005, *Vanig Torikian*
- 137 Out of India, *Lauri Fraser*
- 141 Varanasi, *Christinea Johnson*
- 142 The Raja Ghat, *Charles Lonsdale*
- 143 Varanasi Blues, *Doug Ertman*
- 152 Dream Following Shivaratri, *Christinea Johnson*
- 153 The Cosmic Cave, *Eva Stattine*
- 155 A Night on Cosmic Mountain, *Barbara Jo Fleming*
- 161 The Garland, *Linda Horan*
- 166 Leap of Faith, *Fernando Escobar*
- 168 It's Time to Go Back, *Pat Cookinham*

- 171 Glossary

- 175 About Mark Griffin

illustrations

2	Trident and Seed, *Daniel Hayes Uppendahl*
26	Seed, *Marcelle Marshall*
44	Stone Portal, *Virginia LeRossignol Blades*
46	Rainbow Cloud Samadhi, *Marcelle Marshall*
66	Namah Shivaya, *Marcelle Marshall*
92	The Wave, *Marcelle Marshall*
108	The Ladder, *Doug Ertman*
118	Climbing the Ladder, *Linda Horan*
120	The Voyager, *Pat Cookinham*
165	Commandos, *Mark Bonnlander*

foreword

These are the voices of a few people who have embraced the idea of Total Awakening, the idea that Life carries within it an inherent opportunity for Spiritual evolution.

These stories represent episodes of their passage, the unfoldment of their humanity expressed in journeys across the soul-continent. They may tell of great or small occasions. Either way, the tales represent an experience of human observation.

Life is a risk, a movement, a space! We receive what we make of it! Here is a view into the nature of those whose hearts are risking all. In the spirit of generosity, they share their stories with you. This kind of speech is unique and rare.

Once we glimpse Totality, we can never look away.

Mark Griffin
Founder of Hard Light Center of Awakening
Malibu, October 2006

introduction

I am the worst meditation student ever. When I ask my mind to concentrate with one-pointed attention, it wanders off like a retarded sheep. I fidget. My lack of discipline scandalizes me daily. I certainly didn't get to write the introduction to this book by being a good student. I am, nevertheless, deeply honored to be writing it.

What you hold in your hands is a collection of writings by students of the Hard Light School of Meditation in Los Angeles. The writing reflects us as a group, a sangha—fellow seekers who have gathered together to progress along the spiritual path that ends in enlightenment. The poems, essays, and stories are diverse because we are. We come from all walks of life and many different countries. We're all studying the same thing, yet each of us is having a radically different experience.

What kind of school are we? Just what do we think we're doing? And who is our teacher, anyway?

I would describe Hard Light in dog terms as a terrier—small but feisty, adventurous, ready for anything, focused and determined, stubborn even—capable of clamping down and holding on no matter how we're shaken and stirred. We are intrepid, a hearty band. We travel internationally; we camp in the wilderness; we meditate through heat and cold, by day and by night. We move at a fast pace.

How does it work? Showing up, that's the first thing—you see the teacher and the teacher sees you. And then, without further ado, the teacher silently (or, more amazingly, while he is lecturing) unleashes a maelstrom of energy *inside* you. It swirls around like a waterspout, rushes like a river, submerges you until you are marinating in it. It buzzes around you like a cloud of bees and sticks to you like honey. By the time you go home you can feel it vibrating, ringing in your ears, sitting on your head like a hat. It goes to work on you, all day long, even in your dreams. It changes you.

But really, how does it work? That's a big subject that can fill any number of books, but would quickly overwhelm this slender introduction. I offer instead the following brief, tantalizing explanation that raises more questions than it answers.

Here are six premises upon which our activities are based:

1. The experience of identity in human beings can dilate from a contracted, suffering individual form (I am a person) to an expanded, blissful Universal form (I am Divine).
2. The ability to voluntarily make this authentic evolutionary shift is what we are in meditation school to master; it is the spiritual path.
3. The architecture of the human form is designed to support the Universal state of consciousness, but most people are imprisoned in a contracted identity because their architecture exists in a dormant state, clogged and burdened by the accumulated magnetic force of past actions called karma.
4. Shaktipat is the act of switching on the architecture of the human form, moving it from dormant to active, allowing it to conduct enough energy to generate and sustain the Universal state; this involves awakening the Universal Creative Power called kundalini, and a process called purification, which demagnetizes the burdening karma.
5. A true guru is one who is firmly established in the Universal Identity and can cause others to become so established via shaktipat and purification.
6. Practicing guru yoga means engaging a guru to help you achieve the freedom and ability to switch states of identity from individual to Universal. This is known as forming a teacher/student or guru/disciple relationship.

When students come to meditation class, they are practicing proximity to the teacher, proximity to the force of evolution. Enlightenment is contagious; you can contract it by spending time with someone who has it.

So just what we think we're doing is practicing guru yoga. Yoga is "union," and guru is "that which turns darkness into light," so guru yoga means achieving union with enlightenment. In studying techniques of meditation, we learn how to cooperate with the process of transformation that lies at the heart of guru yoga.

Which brings us to the teacher. Mark Griffin is the Guru-In-Residence at Hard Light. He's an American Guru—honest. He's really American and he's really a Guru. Do you sincerely believe that mastery of

Consciousness is exclusively the domain of Tibetans or Indians? Why *not* an American master? Don't we need enlightenment too? Of course we do, desperately, especially in Los Angeles.

For ten years Mark has been my guru, my meditation teacher, and my friend. I'm exceedingly glad to know him. He takes his teaching duties quite seriously, but lives with playful, down-to-earth humor. He is an ocean of compassion and a fountain of spiritual knowledge and experience. If you inquire with sincerity and respect, there's no question you can't ask. Having him around is invaluable. I love him to pieces.

In the following collection of writings there is a lot of praise for Mark, maybe even some fawning. It should be understood in context. As we receive the grace of shaktipat, each of us feels on some level that Mark is pulling a big thorn from our paw, and we are all grateful. Then too, Love is the language of Consciousness, and that's the language we're learning. The student's love for the teacher is important; the teacher uses that connection to do his work. Enlightenment comes hand in hand with Infinite Love. The more time you spend around the guru, the more it rubs off on you.

Many times I have approached Mark with all sorts of mental goodies: questions to ask, friendly comments to make, thoughts and anecdotes to share, witty banter to engage in. And somehow, within about ten seconds of standing next to him, I am struck dumb. A vortex of emptiness that surrounds him sucks away my agenda, my thoughts, even my vocabulary. In place of these arise an embarrassingly enormous feeling of brotherly love, and a Desire To Stay Very Nearby For No Particular Reason, Indefinitely. Mark takes it in stride that people lose their words near him; I think it happens to all of us. Sangha Speaks, indeed. More like sangha stands tongue-tied, experiencing massive platonic crush!

Here, then, are some thoughts about our teacher, our schooling, and our spiritual journeys that we managed to commit to paper. I hope you enjoy them. If you're intrigued, come visit us to see if Hard Light might be the meditation school for you.

May All Beings Become Enlightened!

Doug Ertman
Santa Monica
2006

THE SEARCH

Spiritual Search: Knowing that there is something infinitely greater than you and seeking it...unendingly.

Trident and Seed
Daniel Hayes Uppendahl

through the looking glass

Lauren Freiman

she walks alone

a black crow
perched on a broken branch in the jungle,
watching the world from the inside

she walks alone

a red star
glistening in a shower of darkness and blinded monotony

she walks alone

barking, howling,
floating across the glass, bottomless floor
in pure ecstasy of the Self

listening for direction
waiting for the knowing
to take her thru the next seemingly clouded layer.

she walks alone

and the water cries
as it washes over the shadow of what she once was
the ocean of mercy
surrounding, enveloping
the one

i will not give up
she screams
i am invincible
and i walk alone
because i am the one and the many

i walk only so that we all may come to know the truth.

Searching for God in Los Angeles

Lauri Fraser

I'd like to say a few words about my search for God in Los Angeles—one of my many searches. It started with a phone call from my friend, Jay. "Hi, Lauri, I've found something that may be of interest to you and your search, an all-day meditation Intensive this Saturday."[1] "Saturday? I'm a hairdresser and it's my busiest day of the week. Besides, I can hardly meditate for twenty minutes, let alone all day!" Everyone sits clearing their mind and all I can think about is global warming and Haagen-Dazs, not necessarily in that order.

I decided to do it. Maybe if I gave my busiest day up to God in the name of "spiritual seeking" then God would make an appearance. He'd owe me one, wouldn't He?

When we arrived, we sat quietly and a young woman appeared and asked that we meditate for a few minutes. Suddenly I felt a strong presence in the room, but I kept my eyes shut. Slowly I squinted them open and there was Mark. He announced that he could talk about meditation all day long but meditation is experiential. "Who among us has never meditated before?" I held up my hand, quickly negating any of my previous attempts at meditating, as it was clear that I was in a whole other league.

I had been on the search for quite some time.

I'm from L.A. Born Jewish, I've never been drawn into any particular religion (including Judaism). Where was God? I was drawn to astrology at age thirteen. At age 20, when life seemed really tough, I got a Buddhist Gohonzon (an altar in a box with Buddhist scripture) and chanted for God. I went to the desert looking for God and found mescaline. Went back to the desert with the Indians looking for Spirit. I went with a friend to see a "saint" and stood in line for over two hours to be blessed and perhaps given the magic words to connect me to the Almighty. I saw psychics and healers and visited holy places. I looked for God in lots of different places, including my own altar in my home. I wanted some answers as to why my life wasn't going better and why the world was

---

1 An Intensive is a day-long meditation consisting of four classic meditations. Mark, the teacher and founder of Hard Light, gives a discourse between sittings.

going into the toilet. If I'm a good person and good people are doing good things then where the hell is God?

Mark gave us specific instructions after teaching us the "Bellows Breath."[2] "Pretend you have a clear piece of fishing line," he said, "and thread it through one ear and out the other. Then take another piece of fishing line and thread it through the center of your forehead and out the back of your head. Next, take another piece of line and tie a knot at one end and string a beautiful deep-blue multi-faceted jewel at the other. Now where the two lines cross, drop the line with the jewel on it down through the top of your head and let it reach as deep and as far as you can until it hits the bottom of your sternum. We will be meditating for about twenty minutes."

I looked at my watch. It was 9:50 a.m. When I opened my eyes and looked at my watch, it was 11:20. Where did I go? What happened?

He had given my mind something to do. I didn't know that then. I know that now. That was fifteen years ago.

It was not until I met Mark Griffin that I started to feel the presence of God in my life. He has taught me how to live in the city in meditation! How to live in my life in meditation. How to avoid oncoming Karma (even if you don't have Karma insurance). Many of my questions have been answered. I constantly find more questions and Mark consistently remains my beacon of light. Along with, of course, Haagen-Dazs. ◯

---

2 The bellows breath is a pranayama meditation breath technique.

Truth

Johanne Joseph

I search for answers among foolishness
I paid no heed to the wisdom of time
Would that I were dumb not blind
For my own cunning shall be my demise
Would that I were brave not shy
Then, the right questions would have been asked
I have sought a long time
Fear always at my heels
Would that I had enough time
I cannot afford to indulge
If I blink, I will miss
The daring that is inherent only in ignorant youth
To go down the rabbit hole and emerge
On the other end of adulthood regret-less
No bitterness, no anguish
Only truth to behold
Certainly not the kind of thing I would deign
To fathom, unholy, untrue
Truth without a veil.

Steps to Liberation

Nadia Marie Harding

> Antonin Dvorak's "Rusalka" was and still is my favorite opera. The story is based on Christian Anderson's fairy tale, "The Little Mermaid," where a water nymph falls in love with a prince. Rusalka, the mermaid, pulls a Faust-like move and gives her soul, her family, her beautiful voice to the witch, Jezibaba, who turns her into a human. When her father Hastrman, the Water Spirit, finds out, he sings a beautiful aria in Czech lyrics expressing the deep sadness over Rusalka's decision and action. She exchanges immortality, freedom, unconditional love, and joy for a desire-based reality, which will eventually act as a pure poison. She was enchanted by a spell that cast her into the human body with feelings of sorrow, suffering and aging.

Ever since the age of 10, I felt disconnected from the body, like I was under a spell. I wasn't able to hold onto anything that felt real. I had a deep belief that there was a power behind existence but I couldn't grasp it. Time moved on. I was still searching for the real thing to enter my life. Dating left me feeling empty. College left me with unanswered questions. Immigration left me searching for a place to belong. Marriage left me searching for true love. Success in business left me searching for more in life. Three children left my bank books empty. Divorce left me feeling alone. Meditation left me striving for deeper meaning. Forty years of my life was over and I still hadn't found that "real thing" I could touch and experience. Still my belief reminded me that there was a major powerful force in existence behind all life. This deep belief propelled me to start crossing bridges.

I began asking for a spiritual teacher who could guide me, was available, close and personal. A few years later, I was introduced to Mark Griffin and the Hard Light Sangha. I received shaktipat[3] and for a few more years I was just cruising through life. I went to meetings and did the spiritual practice. I was observing that little by little my perception was entering a new level of understanding. Things changed drastically for me when Guru Mark Griffin took the Hard Light Sangha to India. We made pilgrimages to sites where Avatars and Spiritual Masters walked, lived and practiced. The sangha camped at the Ganges River during Kumba

---

3 Shaktipat is the descent of grace that awakens the kundalini.

Mela[4] 2001. I was praying for further unfoldment. The prayers were heard.

> *The prince's devotion to mutant Rusalka was challenged by a foreign princess' presence. Rusalka was now experiencing human emotions which she couldn't express. She felt the pain of deception and her heart was broken. She questioned her identity as a human and begged her father, the Water Spirit, Hastrman, to take her back into the divine spirit realm and help her. Unfortunately, that was not the deal Rusalka made with Jezibaba.*

A few months after returning from India, a freak accident happened at Wilderness Boundary[5] during a four-day meditation retreat. The injury left me with scars and nerve damage. Besides physical pain, I felt deceived, unloved, trapped, frustrated and lost. During the year that followed, daily, I was facing my inner blocks, my karmic tapes. I experienced the evil poisons of anger, resentment, revenge, blame and prejudice. Every time my mind grabbed onto one of the poisons and started to plan an action, I was able to look and see the roads and probabilities where the action would take me. I was seeing my mind on one hand and spirit on the other. I found myself in severe chaos and at the same time I was observing all that was happening. I made up my mind to remember the spiritual laws and teachings. I knew that in order not to create any more karma and to start stepping out of the Wheel of Samsara,[6] I needed to be very centered and stay in the spirit. In all the emotional torture I experienced, there was a realization that I could take this really difficult and painful physical experience and create a positive effect. I chose not to wake up another karmic scar. Shankara says in the *Crest-Jewel of Discrimination*, that karma in motion cannot be stopped; it has to be lived. I knew this was an opportunity to change my patterns of reaction, unfold my layers of illusion and make one more step towards my liberation. All this was possible with the gods' Grace, Guru, Lineage and Shaktipat.

---

4 The Kumba Mela is a great roving spiritual festival that has moved among four sites in India for more than 4,000 years.
5 Wilderness Boundary, located in the Sierra Mountains, has been a frequent retreat location for the Hard Light Sangha. The location provides "interesting" challenges to the students as it's at 10,000 feet in elevation and lacks the basic amenities of home or even a poor motel—running water, heat, and bathrooms.
6 Samsara or the Wheel of Samsara refers to the objective world, the eternal cycle of birth, suffering, death and rebirth.

> Rusalka believed she had failed as a human because she was, at heart and soul, a water nymph. She failed because she did not see that the Earth is a free-will planet and there are wide ranges of possibilities and changes are possible. Rusalka drowned herself. Her spirit returned to the water to lure her former lover to his death by a chilling kiss. At the time Rusalka was created, the doors and windows to spiritual knowledge were closed. Humans and other sentient beings had little or no chance to make a difference in their lives. If Rusalka knew that she could find a Guru with a Lineage, receive shaktipat, do the practice and stay in her spirit, she could work off her karma and regain back her immortality.

I can see that because of my spiritual practice I am able to accept more of the Divine Light and continue to refrain from self-destructive reactions.

Finally, I am able to call off the search for that great power behind existence. Every day there's newer, deeper understanding, new discoveries, amazing transformations and clearer perceptions of life. ✺

A Mystery

Anonymous

A mystery only to those
who don't know the way
to remember
Heaven on Earth.
Like remembering
your birthday
a few moments
after dying
when the sweeping breath rests
before grace beckons the next inhale.
And they all wondered why
she kept wailing out loud.

Listening

Wanda Rhodes

Moon is full, sun sleeps,
clouds, stars, timeless sky—at dawn.
Eternity speaks.

Pursuit

Bob Schulenburg

Any gesture of pursuit
Can only be a movement
Away from what is
You cannot ignite something
When it is already burning
Witness the ever-present miracle
Discover/dissolve yourself
In its unending flames
There is not anywhere you can go
And not find yourself
Already there

THE GURU

Guru: The word Guru is comprised of *gu (darkness)*, the formless hidden power of God, and *ru (illumination)*, the beauty and luster of living beings. The Guru is a teacher or Guide to spiritual illumination.

Letter to the Guru

Dr. Shanta Shirset

I have great regards for this mega mountain guru. He is a steady fragrant fountain of Love and wisdom; thy grace is Guru Mark. You are endowed with enormous power which keeps you in the center of all forces. While expressing my deep reverence to Guru Mark I wish to reveal and share that unique experience, realized once in my life, which was hardly of few seconds. While meditating with our group under Guru Mark's influence, in a place away from LA City, in a remote suburb, surrounded by thick forest, a huge bright flash of high energy light emerged and I felt as if I have experienced a fraction of enlightenment filled with great joy. This was the greatest moment I try to think of and would like to repeat, to get back to it but could not for a second time. This was due to pure holy Mark Guru and that holy place which has made a permanent impression on my mind. I feel highly grateful to Guru Mark because of whom I would experience such unique phenomenon. I do express my sincere thanks to my dear friend Astrid who actually introduced me to Guru Mark. Let our Guru enjoy a healthy, long fruitful life to guide our group to elevate all of us to a higher level. With deep love and regards to Guru Mark, Ms. Lee and best wishes to all members.

Loving,

Shanta
Mumbai, India

Meeting the Guru

Ann Brockway

Meeting the Guru: San Francisco intensive

The initial capture was made with a compelling impression: OK—this guy really knows what he's talking about. And it was clear that in intensives, meditation wasn't "nothing;" in spite of inexperience, loss of faith, and a host of obscuring qualities, meditation was "something." My hopes arose.

Meeting the Guru: India—Ganeshpuri and the Yatra[7]

Most of this experience still remains in a place beyond words...but love and gratitude were born there: the Guru was unveiled. It's fully arresting (inner stand-still) to experience a person in full light and power operating in the role of the Guru. Then to be inducted and held in the golden river of the lineage, and introduced, one after brilliant other, to some of those completely at home in God. How I would like to join them!

Meeting the Guru: the schism is displayed

First was the good news, and now the bad news: fully brilliant beings are rare and there's active opposition. A wrestling match begins that includes melodramas beyond belief. The Guru, though still friendly, is looking like a football coach willing to do some serious butt-kicking. Well, OK. There's also some serious support being given and given again and again. A deep trust is being born—and this is new.

Meeting the Guru: the Vajra[8] Guru

Even though the arena is so personal, it's just as true that it's not personal at all: action has reaction, whining doesn't help—that's just how it is. Unfathomable mystery is intrinsic. We do the container, God does us.

Victory to all Gurus!

✪

---

7 A yatra is a spiritual journey to sacred sites.
8 Vajra is a Sanskrit word meaning both *thunderbolt* and *diamond* and refers to a symbol important to both Hinduism and Buddhism.

My Teacher—Guru Mark

Astrid Cheney

Thinking of Mark makes my heart feel full of joy and peace. Immediately. It is just like that. So—what is it that sets off this chain reaction in me every single time? Well, there is more to it than I could describe with the few words here. How did I even meet this wonderful guru? Around ten or more years ago my dear friend Karen told me about a new teacher on the block, Mark, whom I just needed to meet. The first time I saw him, that was it. Powerful, not swayed by appearances and ego, full of an adventurous spirit, humor, and all encompassing love. That was what I was looking for and to top it all off, his message was part scientific, non-dogmatic, and utterly exploratory. I could not believe it; it was all in one package. So—I stayed with it, going to sit with him on the mat as much as I could, absorbing wisdom.

People would come and go in my life, but Mark stayed, always welcoming me, always there to teach me something new. Learning it, digesting it, pondering it, working on it and the cycle repeating over and over again. Just so beautifully simple, it defies any worldly logic. Through the years, I began to value this grace more and more. Mark makes it so easy. I don't have to be anything or anybody; I can just be there and feel the teachings dripping into my brain. Energy is pouring all over me, old concepts fall away and often I don't even know how it happened.

Then, there is this beautiful trust that Mark radiated into me over the years. I just trust him and the unfolding process of enlightenment. He planted the seed or seeds and they started to take shape. I am still totally at the beginning but I just trust the path and method and teachings to bring me where I need to be.

Mark teaches me life lessons. He sets the stage for a certain clarity of mind. Just the places we go—the surroundings are always impeccable, whether it is in the middle of the desert or the meditation hall or India. It is not so much where we are but what a place becomes. You feel the spirit. No sloppiness is allowed. That goes for the language, the setting, the music, the joyful seriousness in everything. It is just plain beautiful.

Mark himself teaches us impeccability in the way he prepares an event, his honesty, his deep thought-out knowledge and understanding and by keeping us all on the highest level we can function. It is something else when I consider how long I have been coming to meditations and what changes we all went through.

On the spiritual level Mark is truly my Guru. It is wonder after wonder I come across by hanging around him. There are little lessons and big life lessons that make me feel I am in the stream of this consciousness. Little lessons start often when I want to see Mark. Hassles start building up, often days before, and I watch them being eliminated one by one. This strange phenomenon can stretch time, can build momentum and energy. The final point is that my intent was to show up and it will just happen against all odds. But this little focus has a much broader ramification. I learned to be a lot more careful with what I want or want to get done. My intentions have to stay clean. I need to step up to the plate, show integrity and work on good, solid goals.

Another point I want to make is that I like this inner peace that often now creeps into my system. People come and go, tragedies come and go, happy feelings come and go, wonders come and go, but here I am—sitting (next to the Ganges?) totally at peace within and around me. Things might go on in the background, people chatting in the distance, a light wind keeps everything flowing, but here I am—sitting. This particular picture has a history relating back to a time Mark was sitting next to the Ganges when we came back from one morning meditation, chatting and laughing. Mark was sitting there totally at peace with everything and all. At times I feel like just sitting there with him, totally at peace. Nothing to be said or done. Just be. Where does this new-found peaceful feeling come from? I credit this to my Guru Mark. A new way of teaching me from soul-to-soul and me wanting to listen. Absorbing the freedom in the fibers of my being. No words, but much joy, deep peace and happiness. And so it continues.

Thank you, Mark.

Your student, Astrid Cheney

(P.S. Hmmm, and let's again change some tires on the road.)

Reflections of Self

Wanda Rhodes

Voice of the Guru,
Grace beyond comprehension,
Love without limit. ✪

The Mystery of Shaktipat

Bart Walton

The advertisement in *The New Times* was bold:

> "Mark Griffin, enlightened meditation master... experience of shaktipat...awakening of kundalini...etc. "

I was skeptical. I mean, I've made it a point to know who's who in the "spiritual world" and have sat with many of the masters and saints living on the planet today. I had never heard of Mark Griffin. "Who is this guy," I thought, "and if he is an enlightened master, *why* haven't I heard of him?"

The photo of Mark Griffin in the ad was a little out of focus and not particularly flattering. To be brutally frank, he looked kind of goofy. I tried to feel put off, but this simple "home made" ad actually attracted me and I kept turning back to read it again. Slick advertising often reveals a "career" teacher who's selling a point of view. That's not to say there's anything wrong with making a career out of teaching. But over the years of meeting a number of remarkable people, I have observed that the real knowers of reality do not seem to be offering a point of view and are definitely not interested in teaching as a career path.

For whatever reason, my curiosity got the better of my skepticism and I decided to attend the free introductory lecture that evening. I entered the meditation room to find a group of people sitting quietly. There was a hushed atmosphere in the room with Mark Griffin sitting off to the side and near the front. He is a big man; his face is strong with hair pulled back in a ponytail. My immediate impression of him was that of a lion. I noticed an empty chair next to him and thought this would be a perfect opportunity to get acquainted with his energy. Over the years, I have learned how to "read" people's energy and find this an accurate way to get a sense of who they are and whether I want to spend time with them. I sat down next to Mark and closed my eyes, waiting for the talk to begin and to get a "read" on his energy.

Almost immediately, I felt a wave of delightful energy tingling at the base of my spine and moving through my body. It was strong and unmistakably positive. Astonished, I opened my eyes and looked at Mark. He nodded and smiled, acknowledging the hit of shaktipat that I had just received. That was my first experience with Mark Griffin.

The remainder of the evening, Mark spoke eloquently about shaktipat, kundalini and the Siddha Path of Enlightenment. This tradition uses the natural structure of the human body (and subtle bodies) to open the channels of Shakti or Cosmic Energy and thus allows the aspirant to experience his or her true nature as just that, pure Cosmic Energy. This is the enlightenment experience seekers from times immemorial have spent lifetimes in search of. The blockages to the Cosmic Energy, on the subtle levels of the body, also manifest as tendencies in the mind which keep the awareness locked in dualistic relationship with the objects of the world. When these blockages are dissolved, the natural Cosmic Energy moves freely through the body producing a feeling of bliss and well being. At the same time, the mind is free to realize a oneness with all that is and a new understanding of Self. The mind realizes its false assumption as the subject of experience and the doer of action. With the blockages removed, the mind is able to see its proper position in the scheme of things, as an instrument of Cosmic Energy in the world and not the real subject of experience or the doer of action. This realization is a concrete observation and not merely an intellectual idea or belief.

This is one path among many respected and effective methods of realizing the truth of who we are. What I find interesting about this method, and what makes this type of path somewhat unique, is that it takes place on the level of the body and does not require mental or emotional effort. The intense flow of Cosmic Energy through the master is enough to trigger a similar flow through the aspirant. All the aspirant needs to do is to show up, be open and quiet.

Mark Griffin definitely qualifies as a master in this Siddha Path. The energy flowing through him is intense and palpable in his presence. He speaks with a profound authority about the mechanics of enlightenment, as well as the tradition of masters before him who act as a conduit of Cosmic Energy through him and into those around him.

Mark was studying as an artist and musician in San Francisco in 1976 when he met Swami Baba Muktananda at the Oakland Ashram for Siddha Yoga during Muktananda's second world tour. Immediately, Mark recognized Muktananda as his Guru and began an intense period of meditation and study with the Indian sage for the next 6 years. In 1982, around the time of Muktananda's passing, Mark went into "Nirvikalpa Samadhi," a deep state of absorption into the bliss of union with Divine

Consciousness. This state of Samadhi was deepened and stabilized during his subsequent six years of study and association with the Tibetan Buddhist sage, Kalu Rinpoche.

After my experience of shaktipat at the introductory lecture, I signed up for the daylong Meditation Intensive scheduled for the next day. The Meditation Intensive is exactly that: intense meditation. After a few brief remarks about the purpose of the event, Mark led the group through four periods of meditation, about $1^1/_2$ hours each, with short breaks in between. The Meditation Intensive is the main vehicle through which Mark Griffin communicates the experience of shaktipat or Cosmic Energy being released through the body. It is simply a period of quietness during which the master and aspirants remain sitting still together. This gives the Cosmic Energy an opportunity to open the subtle channels of the body, which is experienced as shaktipat, or the awakening of kundalini. Without trying to be dramatic, I can say that the experience is genuine and profound. During the intensive, I felt warm energy at the base of my back flowing up my body and filling my head like a balloon. It is blissful and at the same time, very intense. Yet, at no time did I feel unstable or out of balance. On the contrary, I felt a strengthening and a stabilizing power on all levels of the body/mind. "So, this is kundalini," I thought to myself. I had felt this energy before, as we all have in our lives, during times of unusual exhilaration or happiness. But now it was strong and clear enough that I could identify it and know what I was feeling. We sat for most of the day, with lovely music in the background and the delightful flow of kundalini filling our heads. At no time did I feel bored or tired or any of the other unpleasant feelings I imagined I might feel after several hours of meditation. In fact, I could have continued all night, and was sorry when it was over.

Since my first experience, I have attended another Meditation Intensive and remain enthusiastic about Mark Griffin and his work. He is a genuine meditation master and a custodian of the shaktipat as given to him by his master, Baba Muktananda, and Baba's master, Sri Nityananda, before him. A sincere seeker of enlightenment would be well advised to meet Mark Griffin and see whether it might be appropriate to attend the Meditation Intensive. Whether Mark serves as the Guru or simply an interesting teacher along the path, he will undoubtedly make a unique and lasting impression. ◎

The Good Shepherd

Tunga Nath (Matt Hodges)

One of my fondest memories was watching a horse race on a movie projector in a Pan Am 747, flying over the Pacific in the early 70's. I must have been about lucky seven. Grandpa was treating my Mom and me to my first trip to the land of Pele, Hawaii to visit my Aunt Jan. In the good old days Pan Am gave you a handsome sapphire blue shoulder bag with the planet Earth on it. I was a happy camper sitting next to Grandpa picking my numbers. Trifecta ticket in one hand and macadamia nuts in the other. When the little horses crossed the finish line, the win, show, place appeared on the screen. I smiled coolly and uttered, "I gottom." My Grandpa wiped his pop bottle glasses and I'm pretty certain he replied, "Son-of-a-bitch, you did!" Next thing you know a skinny stewardess came over with a monster bottle of champagne. She popped it with a wink and drinks were on the kid.

I'm pretty sure the inner gambler was awakened in me at that moment in time. Something about watching horse races at 20,000 feet and observing all the happy people gave me that warm bubbly feeling inside.

Back on the mainland I continued to bet the long shots. Paud, my Grandpa, took me to Santa Anita where I won my first 100 bucks on a two dollar exacta. I recall picking a shiny black beauty named Lazarus and another one that had a little jockey wearing a cool lime green jersey. Well, they came in as sure as they came out. Driving out of the lot in Paud's town car, I'm pretty sure he said, "Son-of-a-bitch, you can buy dinner tonight."

Old Paud was known for his loud outfits. He was a cross between Rodney Dangerfield and Archie Bunker. I was fascinated with his card tricks and stories about growing up in Kansas City. He enjoyed taking me to meet all his cronies in the turf club at Hollywood Park. I would be swimming in one of his celery green blazers as I met a rainbow of characters in their sea of pastel sport coats, with racing forms hanging from pockets, and cigars somehow dancing on their lower lips. Don't ask what lavender blazers have to do with "let go," but allow me to explain myself.

This was a time of undiluted intuition and absolute relaxation. It was like being in the Wizard of Oz and skipping down the amber highway. The mind was too pure to fiddle around on the thinking channel. The Emerald City was straight ahead.

As relaxation often has a way of playing hide and seek, the hot and cool brain started to play the game of tug o' war. Chemical warfare was taking place in the crossover from the age of innocence to the young man. I think one day I stepped too loudly on a squeaky board and woke up the sneaky elf mind. Those two-dollar exactas weren't coming in like they use to. Too much thinkin' and not enough sinkin', and winkin' into the "let go." The wizard of Oz became a trickster, and I was thirsty for the real Emerald City.

There was only one way to find it and that was to ask. And just like the good book says, "When the chela[9] is ready, the Guru appears." Whether it's a cool Magnolia breeze or a ton of bricks on your head, it's clockwork, and you have to pay the price of admission and be willing to go on the wildest ride of your life. Thank God I had another card up my sleeve.

One day I asked my Grandpa if he was up or down since he started playing the ponies at age thirteen. He said, "Matty, the gambler always loses; the illusion keeps feeding you and setting you up for bigger defeats." I got my answer. I was to be a spiritual gambler instead. The spiritual gambler has nothing to lose. Through victory or defeat once you're on the Dharma Train, Emerald City is a sure bet. It's up to you if you're on the Lightning Express or the slow boat to China. If you decide to play with the big boys, get ready to hold on to a lightning bolt and learn how to let go. Real "let go" and relaxation. You have to become vulnerable.

The sangha is a gathering of souls traveling down the river of life trying to get safely to the Big Blue. It's a great grace if you have the help of a good river guide. This is the Satguru. "El Capitan." The "Good Shepherd" is the one who awakens the student and shakes him up from his slumber. A Satguru gets the student back to his "let go," no mind. I remember the time when I locked into an open-mouthed trance, gazing at a humming bird out the school yard window, while the teacher was scratching away on the blackboard of concepts. In the school of life you have to question everything but with the Satguru question nothing!

The sangha is a flight school and a car wash. It is interesting that during so many of the tapa washes[10] I was going through internally, my outside

---

9 A chela is a disciple or student of a Guru or sage.
10 Tapa (or tapasya) literally means "to heat up." Tapa practices are austere or ascetic practices which purify the mind and give one control over the senses.

job for many years was that of a street cleaner. I worked with a family parking lot cleaning service, scrubbing oil spots with a deck broom. I can't tell you how many graveyard shifts I sweated out, organizing crews scrubbing sludge, and pushing degreaser through asphalt and concrete. It was purgatory for sure, but when I read that Goraknath the king of all Gurus disguised himself as a street cleaner, I pushed the broom like "Cool Hand Luke." After we built the business up from deck brooms to $50,000 scrubbing machines, we were cutting through places like the Beverly Center like greased lightning, boy!

When you're on the path you do funny things like mentally putting the scrubbing machine in your spine and cleaning house. Guess who's driving? Yep, the Guru. He always has your back. So that's the power-scrubbing phase, and there's always more to clean. Just when you've finished 4,000 stalls and you're headin' for 7-11 for Gatorade, guess what you forgot? The loading docks. But maybe after you clean the loading docks it's time to learn how to fly. The Satguru shows you that learning to fly can often take great patience, endurance, and courage. Or he may just say "What in the hell are you waiting for? Let's fly today."

It's kind of like fishing. You might try a salmon egg on the hook, or try a little Velveeta cheese. Some days you try too hard and get snagged up, other days you may try a nice deep crevice. You find that shiny lure in the back of the box, tie a proper knot, and let her drop. She goes down a little further than you thought, and as you drift off into the warm breeze watching the leaves dance on the trees like silver dollars; sure enough she hits, and "weeerrrrrr" she starts to run. But don't hit the reel too quickly; let her go, and enjoy the ride. It's not every day you have a two-foot rainbow on your line. Bring her in steady, stay loose. Then just when you think you have the two-foot beauty in the frying pan, you know what happens next? You thunk too soon. She jumps off the hook and winks at ya.' The rainbow slips right through your hands because you were thinking of the jackpot, the frying pan, or the photograph.

Well, you can either be a stick in the mud or smile into the sunset and buy your buddies pizza back in town. That's sadhana. You see that watching a little one's face letting go of a balloon in a parking lot is worth more than a thousand books. The Guru is Ganesh if you are iced in on Elephant Island, Antarctica. No ego is too big to melt for the Boss.

It gives me great delight to touch his Lotus Feet and bring that touch to my heart. No words can describe what lands, losses, and victories those Lotus Feet have endured. It's not a subject to talk about, let alone figure out.

In a recent meditation when I was very willing to face death, I asked death, "Who are you? What is your Nature?" It's hard to describe what came in front of me. As my body trembled rather violently, death came in the form of a very arrogant dragon/man. Arrogant isn't a good enough word. It was beyond arrogance and pride. This disdainful thing seemed so lofty and Lordly; it was like Darth Vader a thousand fold. I again asked, "What is your nature?" In that millisecond the overbearing, proud force said very calmly, "Fleeting." My sweaty body immediately became dry and "Mr. Hoity-Toity" became a sweaty little mouse. Something about the "fleeting" took the sting out of death, and I saw what a grasp the ego has on human beings. This pride and arrogance was my mirror.

This ego didn't have to be eradicated or put into line; it just had to be seen. Once it's seen, you can ignore it and not feed it any more attention. I almost felt sorry for it; it was like a madman, or junkyard dog barking at the moon.

It took me so long to realize this. "I haven't surrendered yet." If I can give any advice to anybody, it's don't ever stop surrendering to the Satguru until you totally disappear. "Mr. High and Mighty" will tell you differently until the bitter end. You can't find enlightenment; it will find you, only by the grace of the Guru.

This is livicated to the Satguru and all sentient beings. May you always roll double sixes if in a pinch.

Surrender and be honest. It's overflowing. ☯

Bless the charming gardener

Jason Handler

If a single moon can reflect in a thousand different pools,
Why are we so attached to each other?
If a single breath can pass through countless lungs,
Why are we gasping for air?
If a single bee can feed from a field of wild flowers,
Why do we think our honey is the sweetest?
There are few things left in this world, which can be called natural.
Truth is one of them.
The way we feel
is a direct response to who we surround ourselves with
And I can only say that when I am around you
my experience of life is so completely altered for the better
that it can only be called divine.
Please, I mean only to speak the truth.
Because the truth is simple:
If realization of our sacred nature
is the root
and
Love is the flower
then
I must bless the charming gardener. ✿

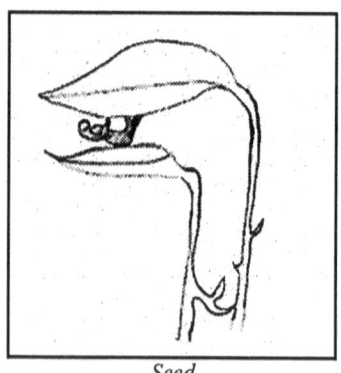

Seed
Marcelle Marshall

The Three Blessings of the Guru

Jeffrey Evan Stamm

    1-000-000-0000

       Hello?

    Hi, may I speak with GOD please?

       Who's calling, please?

    This is Jeffrey Stamm.

       Hold on Jeffrey, I'll see if he's free.

    (Several seconds pass.)

       Hello Jeffrey.

    Hi GOD. Thank you so much for taking my call.

       No problem, how can I help?

    Well, I'm having a hard time finding the right job and I was hoping you might shed a little light on the situation for me.

       I'd be glad to. Have you thought about contacting an executive search firm? I know someone who's really terrific at...

Ever since I was a young man, I always wished that I could call GOD on the phone and speak with him personally. Unfortunately, his number still isn't in my palm pilot; however, I have found something pretty close. I've been studying meditation at Hard Light for over ten years now and one of the most incredible benefits is the opportunity to ask Mark Griffin for some personal guidance.

As an enlightened being, Mark has an innate ability to get to the heart of the matter and help you see things more clearly and honestly. This is not to say that he solves your problems for you or offers specific personal advice. Instead, what one receives is extremely focused and insightful direction on how to find the answer for yourself. How to find your balance so that you can act with wisdom instead of fear. And no matter what the question, the answer is always given with a very powerful and comforting blanket of love. To be honest, most times I have spoken with Mark, it is almost as if the words he was speaking were irrelevant compared to the powerful blast of confidence and hope that I felt in my heart. Perhaps this is because the underlying message I have always received from my teacher is to trust GOD and surrender completely.

Now, receiving personal advice from an enlightened master is truly a blessing, but I have discovered an even more remarkable experience. This one is so bizarre that I don't blame you if you don't believe me. Basically, I have discovered that no matter how depressed or angry or scared or lonely I am when I walk into a meditation with Mark, after leaving, I am so completely at peace and filled with joy that I am unable to even recall what those negative feelings felt like. They simply no longer exist and even the memory of them has been erased. It is truly a miracle to experience a consciousness so pure and elevated that one cannot even imagine what unhappiness feels like. Kind of like eating a five-course Thanksgiving dinner and then trying to remember what hunger feels like.

Unfortunately, Mark's gift of supreme peace and bliss doesn't last, but it is a wonderful snapshot of GOD that allows you to experience the unknowable. How strange it is to contemplate all the bars and nightclubs there are in America, where people go to drink alcohol in the hopes of forgetting their problems and worries. Had they a clue about the bliss of enlightenment, Budweiser and Jack Daniels would surely be replaced with more sublime spirits.

The final blessing of the Guru is the miracle of shaktipat, the mystical seed that, once planted in a human being, activates an extremely accelerated progression towards awakening. Once this wondrous gift has been transmitted, an individual is on their way to universal consciousness and eternal bliss. The irony here is that shaktipat is one of the rarest and most valuable gifts a person can attain and yet it is totally undetectable by any of the five senses. The only way a human being can ever know that they have received shaktipat is with faith alone. Consequently, it is quite difficult to explain this mystery to family or friends, much less motivate someone to actually receive the transmission. I can't tell you how frustrating it is to finally receive this holiest of blessings from the universe and then discover that there is practically no one with whom you can share your joy.

Of course, the good news is that some day, a person in pain will come along who dreams of picking up the phone and calling GOD for help. And thanks to the gift of shaktipat, you or I will be there to answer that call. Someday, a person immersed in anger or fear or depression will sit down to meditate with us and afterwards, know only peace. And someday, each of us will pass this rare jewel of shaktipat on to other souls, until each person searching for GOD's phone number receives an answer to their call. ✺

The Holy Ruby Mine

Eva Stattine

> The great Sufi poet Hafiz said, "Don't die again my friend, with that holy ruby mine inside still unclaimed, when you could be swinging a golden pick with every step."

The first time I sat and meditated with Mark, I felt and experienced a sensation and a light within myself that was so dearly familiar. It was the light that I had seen glimpses of my whole life and had yearned to know more intimately since I can remember; yet up until that moment I hadn't experienced it so clearly and obviously. There has always been a subtle vibration inside me, a longing, a deep curiosity to know what was beyond this mundane existence. Grace has allowed for some incredible books and role models to come across my path, and has given me some amazing life-altering experiences that have increased that subtle vibration and brightened the light inside to help me see the world and myself more clearly. Every step of the way a picture was being painted, and the more I opened my eyes, the more vibrant and colorful the picture became. Up until I met Mark, that vibration was a powerful, driving force in my life, but it seemed as though my unclear mind and somewhat clouded eyes kept me from experiencing it fully. The first time I sat and meditated with Mark was the most moving and refreshing event and no adjective or metaphor could ever do it justice. It was clear to me that it was the beginning of the deepest and most profound relationship I could imagine; the relationship with my highest self, with my Guru, with God.

When Mark came into my life so did a discipline and regular exposure to higher and higher states of consciousness. Mere glimpses of the light were just not enough anymore. As I sat and meditated with him regularly it was as though, over and over again, he would shine a bright light into my Holy Ruby Mine and say, "This, dear one, this is Reality." That bright light allowed me to glimpse beyond my mundane existence and beyond my conditioned mind into the ecstatic equilibrium or a place where the Truth is unclouded. Since then I have not seen the world, nor myself, the same. As my internal reality becomes more illuminated, so does my external reality. Instead of my external reality being something that is separate from me and distracting, it has become a continual reflection of me and what I need to look at within my own life. The light continues to shine through my conditioned mind and shows me what IS, instead of what I want it to be.

Being able to meditate with Mark regularly and being encouraged to have a daily meditation practice has given me a much needed discipline. It has brought me into line, into my center, into a space where I can more efficiently operate out of the present moment rather than being scattered into the future and past. There is a tremendous sense of responsibility that has arisen from no longer operating as much from the conditioned, unaware, or unconscious mind. In the conditioned mind, everyone else is held accountable for my actions, and, in the conscious and aware mind, I am the only one around to blame. So, I've been beckoned to stand in the Truth unfaltering. It's no longer an option to not speak the truth or to think that I'm kidding anyone by being a certain way or not…because everything is on line…everything is seen by my highest self, by my Guru, by God. Because it has become glaringly apparent that All is One, there is no longer anywhere to hide. Anything out of line with the Dharma and the Truth either falls to the wayside or starts creating major conflict until it is reconciled and dealt with. Anything that I am not being completely honest with myself about just keeps tapping on my shoulder or showing up over and over again, and will continue to until I am done playing that particular game.

It has been the most empowering revelation to understand that I have no greater purpose than to continually develop and hone my relationship with Truth, Love, my highest Self, my Guru and with God. Having that purpose in the forefront of my mind has made all of the mundane details of life glimmer with the radiance of Divinity. Knowing that the most precious jewels can be found within the fabric of my own being brings me an unbelievable amount of peace. Embracing the notion that "I" am not my body or this life has made the hard times bearable and meaningful and the good times shine even brighter. Even just beginning the process of surrendering to the Truth and to All that Is and allowing Consciousness to guide me has allowed me to feel an intense sense of protection, come hell or high water, come life or death…because it's All God. No matter how dark or how light, how clear or how screwed up the play may be, it's All God.

When I met Mark, I embarked upon the most irresistible journey, the journey to the center of the Self and to the outermost reaches of the Universe. I met a teacher who is showing me how to swing my golden pick, as well as guiding the way to the Holy Ruby Mine inside. I have been reminded at every stage and step that what I am so hungry for already exists within. It is merely about surrendering to the inner presence of the Divine; surrendering to the emptiness of the space between the breaths and the stillness that rests beyond the mind. It is the Ultimate Adventure! ✲

The Tale of the Mouse

Jeffrey Evan Stamm

My study with Mark Griffin and Hard Light gives my life meaning. At a very young age, I became consumed with finding a way out of the human experience. As an Enlightened Master, Mark has illuminated this pathway with a wealth of intellectual knowledge, precious wisdom, and rare and insightful empirical knowledge. I believe there are only a handful of beings on this earth with the library of awareness he has shared with his students.

I have gained an in-depth understanding of the human architecture and how it is truly designed to function. This includes knowledge of the four bodies[11] of a human being, the three rivers,[12] shaktipat and the Tibetan rebirth process. I understand that the roulette wheel of Karma has more negative experiences than positive, and consequently the odds of producing negative karma are always stacked against us. It is only with the aid of an enlightened soul to mitigate this ever-growing tree of karma, that a soul can even begin dreaming of freedom from the wheel of birth and death.

In addition to gaining a greater intellectual understanding of the enlightenment process from Mark, I also saw him demonstrate the higher qualities of humanity that are so difficult to witness. How does one aspire to be an egoless, loving and compassionate being without ever having met anyone with these qualities? The depth of my teacher's love and understanding fuels my struggle to become a more evolved human being. Before meeting him, it was impossible for me to comprehend the true human potential for goodness and selflessness. Mark has taught me by example and this is the only method with any real value and power.

Because of my deeper understanding of the enlightenment process, I now realize the importance of a teacher and the necessity of proximity. It is only with the gift of shaktipat that an individual's journey to self-realization can begin. I am so grateful for the knowledge and for the grace of my Guru. There is simply no career aspiration that is more important than awakening from this dream and realizing my true self.

---

11 The four aspects of the human form are: the physical (material) body, the subtle (energetic) body, the causal (mental) body and the super-causal body (Atman).

12 Ida, Pingala, and the Sushumna form the three rivers; the three main energy channels in the subtle body.

Thanks to Mark Griffin and Hard Light, this dream that I have carried since childhood has been nurtured and strengthened and my hope of achieving enlightenment has grown stronger each day.

When I came to Hard Light, I carried with me years of religious training in the teachings of Judaism. There was no emotional or intellectual connection to this path; only strong family and cultural pressure and the fear of the unknown. Hard Light is such a drastic difference from this empty religious training. However, there was one over-riding commandment that Judaism had burned into my brain. "There is only one GOD and one must never bow before anyone but Him." I learned quickly in my spiritual studies that this concept was the direct antithesis of the Guru principle. One of the main benefits of the Guru is that he affords the student the opportunity to have a personal experience with GOD, by exemplifying the higher qualities of love, compassion and selflessness. My Guru, Mark Griffin, allows me to experience a much more dynamic and intense relationship between myself and my GOD. Before Mark, my only sense of GOD was born of fear. However, it was still very difficult for me to accept my teacher, my Guru, totally and reject the one omnipresent law of Judaism. This conflict was borne out during our retreats, when students would bow before our teacher and receive Mark's blessing. There are biblical stories of Moses refusing to bow to any man and these reverberated in my head. When I approached Mark for my blessing, I never bowed before him.

One day, at an intensive, we had been sitting with Mark in meditation for several hours. His chair was placed on a wooden stage that rested about two inches off the ground. Suddenly, in the middle of the meditation, a tiny mouse wandered across the floor of the stage and stopped directly in front of my teacher. Mark was deep in samadhi and unaware of our visitor. The mouse stood up on his hind legs and stared at Mark for a while. Then suddenly, his legs collapsed and I watched him fall over backwards. He lay dead at the foot of my Guru. Mark came out of nirvana and expressed compassion for the little mouse that had found his way to an enlightened Master and joined our intensive. Mark told us that the little guy had received a fatal transmission of shakti that had simply blown out his physiology. He expressed respect for the mouse's final gesture and explained that the tiny creature would receive a much higher birth on his next incarnation. The little mouse was placed in a shoebox, a prayer was said and he was buried behind our center.

At the next retreat, one student after another walked up to Mark and bowed before him to receive his personal blessing. I bent my knees, lowered my head and bowed in loving surrender to the touch of my teacher. ✪

I Breathe for My Guru

Tim Maloney

Hi. My name is tim maloney. I am a human being. My guru's grace has made it so. I had been given an AIDS diagnosis and was living in a descended state of existence for nearly two years, a subhuman, a martyr, an AIDS Victim. I hated myself and every other diseased human being on the planet and I never stopped myself from the spiral I had created, which descended into a hell of no redemption. Instead I embraced it. Embittered, determined for my demise, I acted out my hate for the world through my sexual addiction. I was sick and dying when I found my guru by chance through the fate of an astrologer who guided me to stand on the beach in the early morning hours of a summer's new moon, calling out to the universe, to my God, to show me my destiny...to make it appear because it was time. Within weeks I found my gift, found my breath, found my guru, Mark Griffin.

There are many stories I could convey which illustrate the faith I have been led by through his internal guidance. One is simply put. I had always been a night person and a twelve to fourteen hour sleeper...getting up very late mornings or early afternoons. My profession as an entertainer helped me develop this routine. Within the first year of studying with Mark, I began to get up at 4 a.m., almost on the dot. I was given this internal clock, not by my own desire, but by my guru's grace, to lead me to awakening.

When I asked my guru to take away my sexual addiction, I became impotent within two weeks. This was certainly not what I had expected, but with this decrease in sexual potency, I gradually lost the obsessive thoughts about sex and the incessant need to gratify them and ended up being celibate for almost a year and a half.

When I asked my guru to teach me true integrity, I was blessed to go through AIDS wasting and dementia, which led to delirium and an acting out of my deep-set self-entitlement issues where I found myself in jail on charges of grand theft of personal property. This was after studying with Mark for nearly two years. This was after learning The Four Noble Truths and The Noble Eightfold Path and earnestly living by these tenets. As I look back at the year that it has been since jail and being put in a convalescent home by my family, left to die, I have truly embraced the gift Mark has given me. I believe that this rapid scorching of my karma by Mark is what has propelled these bizarre situations to arise allowing me to process and burn quickly the ills that harbored my hate for the world and myself.

E-Mails to My Guru

May 23, 2002

Dear Mark,

I felt I needed to write you because I forget things when I am in your presence. I am having concerns over feeling like I'm not being responsible.

I am enjoying typing for you. Your words and my fingers seem to be gluing themselves together. It's like magic sometimes. After sitting with you so much and spending so much time on my computer with you as I transcribe your delicious words, I have been having conversations with people that I find surprising because of the amount of information you have shared that I find myself reciting nearly verbatim. I have visions of helping in some way to see that you are published, if indeed that's what you would like. According to some of your lectures, that would be a natural sequence of events. I thought about interning in a publicist's office to learn how to publicize you. I see so many magazines that don't have your information in them and feel you are such a special teacher that I want the whole world to know you. I don't think this comes from ego; I think it comes from the direct experience with you. Knowing that if I can stop hating myself, so many others would benefit in similar ways. I want to write my personal story for the HIV community about my journey going from a death sentence to sitting in bliss with a spiritual master.

December 29, 2002

Dear Mark,

Hi. I was at my acupuncture session with my healer the other day and she said you would like us to write an essay/letter to you and describe how we have improved this year...or how your teaching has affected us. So, I'll begin my story.

I came to the Shankara's *Crest-Jewel of Discrimination* [teachings] in

January, and vowed to never Act again after I realized how I was going about it all from ego, but by the last week of March I did an audition, a singing audition. It was sensational because I finally broke the wheel of fear for myself and meditated a lot before entering the room, becoming very centered, taking the time I needed...not starting just because the pianist started...allowing the space...the sacred space for this singing monologue to happen for the first time. This is the way I used to perform...before the ego got into the act of wanting to know or read the auditors and know exactly how every note I did was perfect. All that crap went away for a moment and I experienced peace, a peace that was so powerful for me. I was happy again.

When I came back to see you after staying away for six or so weeks, you gave me the most incredible guru dream...it was my first Technicolor dream. Where I was on a flying carpet...and where you said in my ear...be the first to follow me...it's made a huge impact even to this day. And I felt as if it was a dream about forgiveness.

Easter and Ojai[13] came and went and was incredible...at least that's what I wrote in my journal. Don't remember it very well, except that I became stronger in my quest to root out my own personal faults, including my sexual promiscuity. And I believe you had given me a guru dream that I was an actor and that I was successful getting a show in Vegas after being heard by a couple of producers. This changed my mind somewhat about leaving acting and I was really confused by it but happy at the same time because I knew I was good at acting and I knew I loved singing, but didn't know how to make it happen without my ego. And yet, by this time I was very much dependent on the Social Security system financially and was torn between feeling well and needing to not feel well so the system could take care of me. Not wanting to take responsibility financially left me in a void because I had no integrity.

Then May 11 came and you gave us the mantra, Om Na Ma Shi Va Ya, and in an instant I was transformed because I had something I could do when I was out of sorts that would bring me back to center and even better than center. I had been given a gift to reach outside of my box. I found myself doing the mantra with the mala at restaurants with my

---

13 Upper Ojai Valley is home to Meher Mount, a beautiful retreat site used by Hard Light students.

friend. He would say I was bobbing...I couldn't help it...I was so empowered with this new energy that I would say, "I can hear you much better and more fully while I am doing this, than if I weren't." I did walking meditations through the swap meets and life became easier. My antisocial energy was being transformed.

Then we went to the Vajrapani Institute[14]...for one of the best experiences I've had to date...I chose to be silent for the three days...and wore my ear plugs so it was easy for me to basically block people out. A few times I had to say, "I'm choosing to be silent." But overall, people were respectful. I had more dreams...guru dreams. This time I was a girl in a beach blanket movie. So, somehow you were showing me that I was going to be successful in acting, but that it wasn't going to be Shakespeare and that that was OK; that I would be doing frivolous stuff. The trip was so great for me...those woods...those trees...that air...the freedom. Thank you for that choice...it was brilliant for me.

I came back renewed and eager to begin my intestinal cleanse...which I did for the month of July. I felt so empowered 'cause I was so good on the diet. I had integrity and didn't cheat myself, which felt so different and good. Then the fast came...and the last week, just after I had finished a week-long fast, I ended up having words with two tenants [in my building]...and a lot of yelling happened...That's when [my landlord] kicked me out.

I decided to go to NYC...to run away and was devastated when I got food poisoning there and when I kept feeling closure everywhere I went. I was saying goodbye to NYC. I didn't want to be there anymore, and I missed my dog, Coco, something fierce. I spent more time thinking about that dog...and how much she loved me and taught me to love others...or was teaching me. I ended up coming home a month later and spending the entire month of October in bed...seriously depressed... until I went back on my meds...and you prayed for me...to Sri Laxmi...and I prayed to her...and then I decided that I missed doing Reiki. So, even though I don't see energy...and I'm not psychic, I feel that doing that is my tithing...and I want to help in that way. As soon as I came to that conclusion I got three jobs in one day, yours included.

---

14 Another site of Hard Light Sangha retreats, located in Northern California.

Well, I started the job at the restaurant but ended up with hemorrhoids. I continued to work though, even on Thanksgiving Day with not only that, but I was unable to urinate. Two days later, way too long, I went to the emergency room and got a catheter and was loaded up with drugs...spent a week totally praying and trying to release whatever I had been holding onto. I watched the church channel [on TV] and prayed to God and Jesus and to you and Sri Laxmi and to Shiva and the Siddha lineage and tried hard to surrender. I had no choice. A tube was stuck in me in the most undesirable place. And surrender I did. By the end of the week, I actually worked a lunch shift with the catheter in. I might be the biggest martyr...truly...but somehow, I was empowered by taking action and living and making the best of things. When that catheter came out, I was a changed human being, treasuring myself in a new way. Respecting myself...And that's when the fifteen days of work happened that brought in my entire India trip money. Unbelievable. I found myself Loving waiting tables, a truly miraculous event. I honored money...I sent some to my Grandmother as a tithe...and the money kept rolling in. I counted it and wasn't afraid of it...and I was just very different at work. I had integrity. So, I feel that the last year has been remarkable for me...a gift from God. I finally am open to receive the blessings God has in store for me.

I am so fortunate to have met you and to have you in my life. Thank you for the opportunity to reflect back on this. I look forward to our future...

Respectfully with peace and reverence,
Your devoted disciple, Tim

July 15, 2003

Please help me with prayers Mark and if it is my karma to live and be a powerful being and help other people here or on other planes, please help me to align with my heart's truth. To have integrity.

September 25, 2004

I became a Christian. I had to choose between the bible, in its current form, or you and believing in reincarnation. It was hard, but I did it. I rebuked you. Then my Reiki Master told me to Bless you for all that you have done and to please release me. I've done that too. And yet, you still persist. My yoga class is consumed by thoughts of this following Guru dream you gave me. I shed tears of Joy because I realize that I think I know what you meant. Maybe I'll hold off on my ideas...I wish you much peace. I had a beautiful cap of energy today while I sat on the beach in Malibu. I realize I may not be with you in the physical form anymore, but your HARD LIGHT is unstoppable. And your unconditional love is felt.

There is an excerpt of one of my letters to you that I didn't send, but told you about. I also told Lee since she was in it. I believe it was sometime in 2001 as it speaks of a Tuesday night class in Oct 2001 where you talked about traveling worldwide. Here is the excerpt.

"My guru dream was great, but it was unclear. You, and I remember Lee being there briefly, presented me with magic gloves. I put them on and found myself directly in front of an old friend who I had a misunderstanding with and an eventual split. I asked her to forgive me and told her about you being an enlightened soul. Immediately my gloves were taken away and I was whisked away by force. You came to me and handed me a ticket or piece of paper and said, 'Be the first to follow me.' I took this as a second chance and was immediately put on a magic carpet where I flew to a world of incredible beauty, more pleasing to each sense than I have ever experienced in this life. I landed and was guided down the side of a mountain where I heard birds singing, children playing, water splashing in the breeze and chanting. As I turned a corner I saw an old man sitting in a carriage type of structure being carried by servants. The woman and children were singing and as I passed I heard them say clearly, 'Who will follow him?' [This is added as I remember it.] I realized you were the old man giving me a test...I said, 'I will, I will' and the old man turned into you."

I don't need a response. I know you're here. Much love and thankfulness for teaching me to know what living in integrity might really mean. By the way, my public defender pleaded not guilty as I was diagnosed with AIDS Dementia. It's not on my ct scan anymore now that I am med compliant. Hard lesson to learn.
Love Tim

September 28, 2004

I am so sorry. Please forgive me. I have been a wicked and malevolent human being. I do not deserve to have you as my teacher. I had to leave you something at the hall. I was too selfish before to give you my finest Buddha. Please accept this. I think of you constantly. Tim

November 19, 2004

You came into my dream a few nights ago...you did that spinning picture kind of thing like on your brochure and you popped up on my computer screen and I recognized you as God and you said, "It's OK Tim, you can go back on the wheel of samsara." Everyone was very loving to me Wed. night...I forgot how strong the light was in each and every member of the sangha. I'm so happy for your new book's success. Love Tim

November 23, 2004

I'm on a pass from the hospital, the psych hospital. I had an allergic reaction to a sleep aid. I was trying to rush out of the hospital because I didn't want to spend Thanksgiving there. I was too proud to do that. My pride was so hideous that I could not even bring myself to tell another person that I had nowhere to go for the holiday. I was truly pitiful. I had such intimate talks with these people, I felt very comfortable, and yet, I thought it would be awful to end up in a psych ward over the holiday. That is until this one wretched-looking crack addict came up into my face and I recognized her as God. And she spoke to me with the words God needed to tell me. I melted. I'm melting. My hands and feet are vibrating like never before. I gave Reiki to two women so far. Not touching, just sending. I have never felt the sparkles of radiant energy like this. I am free. Of my judgment. I read your book in one sitting on Saturday and applied the ideas as I read. If there is any way that you can help me get back into the work force and pay my own way, I would be so grateful to you, Mark. I am ready to cease this spinning and get rid of material things I have collected, so I can focus on Awakening. In the deepest, warmest place, Tim

December 8, 2004

Thank you so much for your book. I am not a felon. There was a good outcome in court yesterday. Your book and the idea about coming to the understanding of what's important and what is NOT, permeated my experience yesterday. In my meditative state doing Reiki in the courtroom, I kept picturing the words that you wrote: to have discernment. I have become an advocate for the mentally impaired...I have an affinity for them. It took some time to drop my fear, but I certainly connect with these individuals. There is something about bringing out a personality in someone who is "dull" and I think of you and how unconditionally you love everyone and how your eyes sparkle and I am finding myself taking on these qualities more and more and it's such a beautiful gift for myself and these other gods. When I was in the hospital I found this ability to draw out conversations even with a catatonic individual. I'm not sure where this will take me...actually if it never goes a day further, I now have shed my fear of other humans and that has been such a great neurosis.

December 14, 2004

I realized tonight as I was driving to class that my path with heart isn't about a job...it's about seeing God in everyone and everything and emulating the heart of Jesus and of you.

A letter written to my acting teacher sometime in October 2005:

Basically, I went into Samadhi, at least for part of the day, on Saturday.

That is a deep connection with all that is...the ocean of consciousness, as my guru says...in that state, and having my guru confirm where I had been, I even told him as he was describing what events led me there, "Who cares...who needs to describe it, I felt it." And briefly shocked my guru with my statement...it was glorious really...basically copying my guru, mimicking his every move, the way his mouth hangs slightly open and his tongue circling slowly, his motion back and forth, a gentle throb urging his gait. I can't say just how much breath I allowed myself to devour and be enveloped by, but it was gallons at a time, so much so that I feel that my body is in shock at descending back into my world.

Stone Portal
Virginia LeRossignol Blades

Teh Teh La La

Nathan Goreham

Teh Teh La La
The Guru shows up at the beginning
ring, ring
smiling bell and existing fingers.

White elephant
Black cobra, with lightning as a tongue.
Cosmic rain.

The black yogi shows up at the end
stomping wrathful bliss.

✪

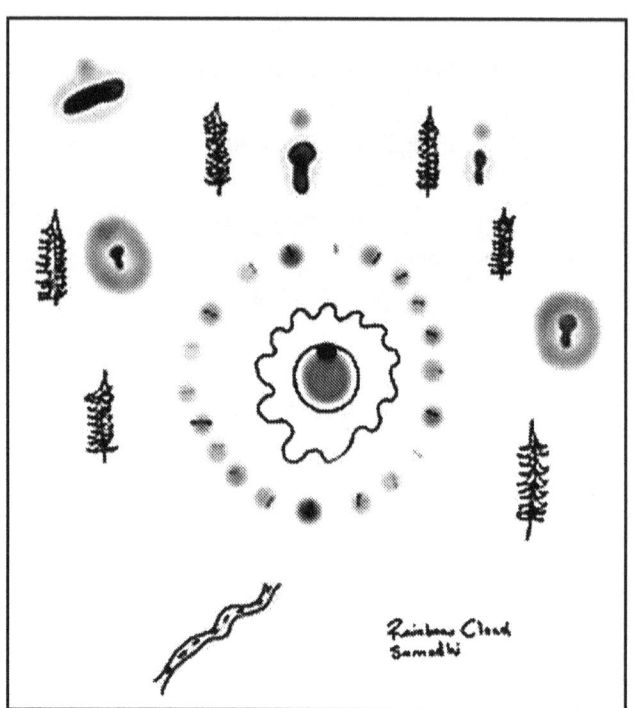

Rainbow Cloud Samadhi
Marcelle Marshall

THE SANGHA

Sangha: *Conventionally, the sangha is the community of spiritual aspirants. Ultimately, the sangha is those beings with experience of ultimate reality or emptiness. These are the High Ones.*

Dear Reader

Eliana R. Farias

Dear Reader,

My name is Eliana. I have been participating in the sangha for about two years; I have been on a conscious spiritual quest for about seven. Throughout my life, there was a part of me that felt that there was more, but I couldn't quite put my finger on what that "more" was or where I could find it. I just knew it was out there. I kept looking here and there, but what I found would never suffice. I kept saying, "There must be more."

It wasn't until I met Mark and started practicing with Hard Light that I finally found a place where I could stay; I had finally found that "more" I had been searching for.

Home at last!

The most memorable day yet at Hard Light was receiving shaktipat through Mark. That day a newer, better and awakened me came to be. It was such an incredible and indescribably amazing experience. I cannot explain it with words. I have not been the same person since. I am so much better. EVERYTHING has been enhanced on every level. I can't explain it or comprehend it at times, but I trust it completely.

Being a student in Hard Light is an exhilarating and challenging experience. Being in Mark's presence is a gift of grace. Never have I been around an individual whose presence could affect me so much. Not only on the physical realm, but in realms I didn't know I could experience. At times, he'll walk around the room to work more individually with each student. As he does I experience things that I simply cannot describe. It is so beyond me. All I can say is that I have finally gone beyond my limited concept of God. I believe I am finally closer to the truth. Answers are finally being expressed, and the best part: I am experiencing them for myself.

The challenging part comes at different levels. Physically, my body had to adjust to the meditation process—in essence, "purify." I had to learn how to still my body, to endure hours and hours of meditation, to surrender to the process. and to go beyond my basic self in order to experience the beyond. It is very difficult at times, but the result is worth it. In addition, so much introspection allowed me to enhance my mind and emotions. Since the emotional and mental realms are so interlinked, mind leading the emotional realm, I have been able to acknowledge and clarify my thoughts—clean house basically—and release anything that does not serve me. As a result, I am a much more balanced and healthy emotional being.

On a spiritual level, everything has accelerated. Each day feels like a hundred lifetimes. Each day is so full. I feel like I am driving at 200 mph in an 80 mph zone. I feel I am processing my karma like there is no tomorrow. I welcome this process. I feel lighter and lighter as I release even though it feels like I'm not going to live through some of it! I experience more and more of who I truly am...a divine being having a human experience. Hence, I am able to participate much more fully in life and live my life with joy and enthusiasm. Each moment is so precious and so abundant with life and Spirit. Never have I felt so close to God. Never have I felt God everywhere all the time. Never has life held so much meaning and each moment so much life.

In a nutshell, the more I meditate with Mark, the longer I am able to maintain this relationship with and to God. Having a place to meditate, people to meditate with, and a leader to guide me has been one of the key findings in my life, truly a blessing and a treasure. Come join the journey, see what you've been missing! ☉

The Hard Light Way

Pauline Arneberg

New Year's Eve; what to do? I knew I wanted to do something different. I didn't enjoy "partying" and wanted to do something that acknowledged spiritual values. In the mail came an invitation to attend a retreat in Catalina. OK, maybe this would be an answer. My husband agreed and we took the ferry to Catalina to discover Hard Light.

The hotel chairs were in a circle; a large black chair seemed to dominate the room; to the left was a table with snacks. People introduced themselves. I remember thinking, "older than I had expected." Mark came in and sat in the black chair; everyone went into silence and, I guessed, into meditation. It seemed interminable; the silence was deafening. I wished Mark would say something. In time, he began to talk. As he spoke, I began to wish for the silence again. I wasn't at all sure what he was talking about; I wondered if everybody else understood him. I waited for him to stop talking. The retreat alternated between long periods of meditation and short talks. By the end, while I didn't understand the language, nor too much of the message, I was certain I had discovered someone who could teach me more about spiritual life.

That was about ten years ago. There have been many moments of spiritual fulfillment; of emptiness, of comfortable silence with no need to do, nor to think, nor to hope. Simple existence—glorious, complete. I've learned some of the language; some of the strange concepts are now friends. I've grown comfortable with meditating an hour a day; with reciting malas;[15] using incense; and frequent trips to India.

I'm not an ascetic; I live in the world and have always searched for a spiritual path that integrates All That Is with the unfolding, evolving, chaotic energies of people and organizations. My involvement in Hard Light has helped me think more clearly about most issues. I now believe we live in a karmic stew, and the wheel of samsara has a ferocious intensity; the choice is to accept or resist the force of spiritual evolution. Often, my mind chooses to resist; what is different, now I see the pain resistance causes me and others.

The regular Thursday meetings often feel like an island of sanity in a world of insanity; learning to give up suffering is not easy. Many, many

---

15 Mala beads are a tool to assist in mantra meditation as they help the meditator maintain focus and optimum energy levels.

day-long intensives and longer retreats later, I still experience joy at the prospect of a day in mostly silence. It is not always a blissful silence; often unknown pain surfaces and I ride the waves. Enlightenment, this lifetime, possible? I continue to commit myself to this goal, yet, I've become more realistic about what is required.

Relationships in the sangha have an intense quality; most people do not come here to socialize. Intense yet detached is how I would characterize the relationships. What we do in the rest of our lives is not discussed much. I've seen people physically change; expressions that were hard, tense, and aloof seem to metamorphose into faces that are peaceful, attractive, warm. I watch people come and go and wonder what takes them away. I often wish for fuller conversation about the meditation experience by the group, but that does not seem to be the Hard Light way. There is a classic Indian relationship between guru and jiva established here. The guru maintains primacy at all times.

There is a fun dimension to all this serious work as well. I remember my first camping experience: I was totally unprepared for what a four-day camping journey involves; it was a jaunt to hell in some ways. I didn't bring warm clothes for the cold evenings; fortunately, someone had the foresight to bring extra warm clothes. I found myself inept at setting up a tent, but someone came to my rescue. Help was abundant. By the end of the experience, I knew I could do it again with more humor.

I remember a trip to Santa Fe; this was my first intensive outside of Los Angeles. The intensive was held in a small, Buddhist temple; the transmissions were so intense I thought my bones would be crushed. Sometimes releasing karma is disorienting—my husband drove down a one-way street the wrong way in an effort to find our hotel. We had breakfast with Mark the next morning. His humor was in full force; he was totally available. I was surprised conversation could be made so easily.

This is Thursday—Hard Light night. I've been away for over a month working. I feel like I am going home; I know I will experience more of my wholeness. ○

Hard Light: Modern Life Meets Timeless Truth

Doug Allen

The Olympics are playing in Athens to seats left empty because of potential terrorism. Presidential hopefuls are in mid-campaign in yet another lesser-of-two-evils election. Oil, religion and power are tossed together in a strange union that has the world on the edge of chaos...

Though the characters and scenes of life's drama change from age to age, the drama itself goes on as it always has been and always will be. The drama of life continues inexorably. Yet as inexorable as this drama is, the unfolding of truth, traveling from master to disciple, from the universal to the individual, is just as unstoppable. This is the Hard Light Sangha. Here, modern life with its travail and travesty, with its joy and happiness, is peeled open revealing something quite unexpected. Here the illusion that modern life is real gives way to new, yet timeless vistas. A new life is revealed, one that always has been and always will be.

Here, the lightning of awakening strikes, moving surely and steadily through the beings of the sangha. The descent of grace, the greatest prize, floods us. Yet, amongst ourselves little is said of it because it doesn't translate into modern conversation. In fact, much of it doesn't even translate into our own consciousness. It happens; we know, because we ourselves are the proof, but how and why it happens is a mystery. It always was a mystery and always will be a mystery. So in the Hard Light Sangha, the casual conversations still lean to the mundane, to the drama of life, to the struggle of living in balance with all the forces that vie for our attention.

The greatest adventure is happening to each of us, but what can we make of it? We watch identity and idea sink into the ocean of consciousness and in those moments allow the timeless truth to settle within us, as us, changing us into what we have always been and always will be. Little is said as we are irrevocably changed, annihilated by love. We acquiesce to the futility of description and let it be.

In Hard Light the modern mind and timeless truth coexist, not as enemies, but as factual and necessary states of being. Perhaps this is Mark's most deft and sweeping maneuver, that timeless truth and modern mind blend into a mutually supportive collaboration. And perhaps nothing shows this blend and balance more than the origin of the Hard Light name: as Mark said, "It sounded cool."

Modern life goes on, as it always has, as it always will. And the timeless truth penetrates it as it always has and always will. And in this moment, I am the witness of this event. I won't speak of it; you just have to experience it for yourself, and it is so cool... ✪

Studying with Mark

Judith Bluestone Polich

It has been almost a decade since I was introduced to Mark Griffin and the work of the Hard Light Center of Awakening in Los Angeles. At that time although I had sampled most of what the western spiritual circuit had to offer and had traveled several times to India to study with teachers widely recognized as great masters, the thought of an eight-hour meditation intensive brought up more images of acute discomfort if not outright agony than the possibility of great and transforming benefit. Fortunately some deeper part of myself took charge. Thus I came kicking and screaming to the door known as Hard Light that Mark so gracefully holds open.

Moving to Los Angeles was out of the question but Mark does not ask a lot of his students. "Come," he said, "sit with me. Commit to an hour a day of meditation at home. Try to make it to several retreats and intensives a year. Let's see what happens."

That seemed reasonable. In those days I lived in Santa Fe and Mark and his followers held several intensives and retreats in the Southwest every year. So one afternoon armed with pillows and enough chocolate bars to keep my resistance subdued, I entered my first meditation intensive. I could not have prepared for what I was to experience. By the end of the day my energy body felt as if it had been chewed up and reconstituted. You could call it a spiritual rebirth but it was some time before I knew where my darkness ended and my light began. To say the energy available in Mark's presence is palpable is a dramatic understatement. I had touched something my conscious mind could not decipher. I had begun a process that was both irresistibly attractive and absolutely frightening.

Up until this time you must understand I had only read about genuine spiritual practice. I understood it all intellectually. I did not really grasp that the spiritual path happened in your body, intentionally and with direction as the kundalini was activated and the path of your life force energy was directed upward one chakra at a time. I had been on one spiritual path or the other for years. But Mark teaches the path of kundalini meditation. He says there is only one path, the one that runs from your root chakra to your crown chakra. Over time I learned what a guru is and began to grasp what a committed meditation practice offers.

Mark was an art student when he met his teacher, Swami Muktananda, in Oakland, California in 1976. Some eight years later when Swami Muktananda made his transition, Mark entered a state of awareness known as Nirvikalpa Samadhi. This state, described as absorption in blissful union with divine consciousness, was deepened and stabilized for Mark when he subsequently studied with Kalu Rinpoche, a renowned Tibetan master. Sometime later Mark began to give shaktipat.

Shaktipat is an energetic transmission of powerful cosmic energy that flows through and opens the subtle energy channels of the body, awakens the flow of kundalini and plants the seed of divine union. Mark also began to offer the Siddha path teachings known as the path of Rising Sun. The Siddha lineage of the Rising Sun that extends from Mark to his teacher, Swami Muktananda to his teacher, Sri Nityananda, is a lineage based on direct transmission from teacher to student. It is not only the most enduring but the brightest and clearest shining light that is present on our planet.

As I began to commit to a meditation practice I came face to face with what Mark describes as our darker angels. I witnessed that Mark carries the presence of the guru, the energy of a holder of an ancient and powerful lineage of light. I saw how contact with the presence of the guru flushed out both my dark side and my light. The great insights and heights of a meditation retreat were often followed by deep rifts and rages, peaks and valleys. As Mark says, "the guru's light goes to the depths of an issue at all times." There is no holding back once you receive shaktipat and put yourself on a path. Gradually even slow learners like myself come to understand the path is the teacher. There is always choice. The task is to stay in awareness and choose consciously; to choose where we put our attention. The path teaches us to use the skillful means and consciousness of love that Mark so clearly articulates. We need to learn to consciously choose the higher angels.

My life has dramatically changed since I first received shaktipat from Mark. He is remarkably kind and an exceedingly generous person. He holds great integrity. There are very few teachers who can equal Mark's ability to so cogently and clearly articulate the intricacies of the inner states of consciousness in a manner that Westerners can understand. I consider myself very blessed. ○

Light, Love, and Emptiness

Fernando Escobar

"How are you this morning?"

> "I have been busy working on a new project with my business and doing real well. I'm finally getting the clients I need and making some money. I got to see this big house I'm selling. It has a big commission so my wife and I can move. How've you been?"

"You know, getting things together and studying daily and working out..."

> "Yeah, I've been working out too but haven't read any books lately. My wife hasn't found a job yet but I like having her at home."

"How is she doing, I haven't talked to her for a while. She called me to see what I've been up to..."

> "She is doing well but not working yet because I might get this big house in Laguna Beach, start saving up for my own company, and retire as soon as I can to travel with her and my dog."

"Sounds great, so how soon are you looking to move since..."

> "Maybe Laguna Beach or Newport Beach. I haven't decided. As soon as I sell a few houses in a month, we'll be all set to go and get out of this area. It's beautiful down there and peaceful."

This is the typical conversation I have every day with virtually everyone, in different situations, about different subjects, in the same context. Emptiness. Nothing is really said. We just talk about ourselves to ourselves and others consistently to believe the story we're telling. Like a test to see if what I say to others will heighten my importance in this life compared to others. As if the race will always continue and getting ahead is the best way to overcome whatever is chasing us. I witness how everyone I meet and interact with tries to get in as many words about "I" as much as possible. To show the other how good we are at grasping and holding on to an imagination; having the best ropes and equipment so that nothing will let me fall from the edge of this rock. "Look mom, no hands."

Every day I see less. I see less in myself to want to hold on to, an imaginary edge that slowly loses its existence. And I see how others tie their ropes to everything and anything, into their very own existence. How about reaching for something real? Whatever happened to talking about something that is *real*, and I mean real substance. Ideas and conversations of what is truly *real* compared to all of the nonsense of impermanent existence. Suddenly I stepped into the Hard Light.

Finally, a group and a teacher with real conversations of substantial existence. The light is made of the most solid substance I have found yet. In fact no need to search any further. Just holding on to this hard light and allowing it to give me momentum towards true existence is my understanding of Mark's teachings to me. It is never about "I"; it's all about what is really taking place here, right now. Putting my thoughts aside and looking down at the waters from this imaginary edge. Letting go to a vastness of truth and being so lucky to have someone come along and let me know that the water is warm. The more I give in to the free fall, the easier it is. Once in, I'll never know the meaning of freedom.

Mark Griffin opened my eyes to what love really is, can be, and will be. To surrender to *true love* is meditation. Like a pregnant woman, I have felt a growing presence within me since my first day of shaktipat. It must be my senses looking inward to what really lies deep within me, focusing every day on what I can find. Meditating, meditating, and meditating on this one point. It must be love because Mark says that it is the only thing that exists; everything else is emptiness. So if my interaction with another human being has no love then nothing has happened. No sparks, no sharing, no love. Just a game of taking and more taking; no giving. Only listening to when the other can get the next word in about their own identity. Yet I do have moments with a select few that I share and strive to reach the ocean of consciousness.

What I witness is that everyone indirectly wants to be in the ocean of consciousness. They wish to be with love and receive love every day. But love is identified with material objects or other beings we have relationships with. The decision to be with God at all times is not the common goal of the majority of the population. Being in Hard Light is making that decision and confronting the behavioral patterns that create a barrier between me and God. To have the obstruction was my idea and to release it is in my power.

Mark has taught me more than I could imagine in this life. He lets me see what it would be like without any obstacles; it's up to me to decide to transform the patterns that make me less of who I am. I am "This and That" and not the negative patterns of my limiting identity. Not only does Hard Light help in bringing to awareness the *true love* that waits but also the illusions I have created. Hard Light is the opportunity to get the work done now. Of not waiting for the next life to be with God—especially since I have a guide to take me through the dark deep forest to the beach of the *ocean of consciousness*. ⚙

Don't Come—You Wouldn't Like It

Bob Schulenburg

I would like to take this opportunity to lie to you about the sangha. I would like to tell you about how unremarkable and mundane it is and how plain and ordinary and bereft of magic or mystery. I would like to encourage you to not be interested or to think there is nothing to gain by coming into contact with it. It is just a slightly odd collection of plain simple folk, inclined towards delusion, evolving around some large good-natured American guy who likes to either sit there and say nothing for hours at a time or go on and on about Shakti and kundalini[16] and the Sushumna[17] and the grace of the guru and what a big deal it is to come into contact with it and how, someday, if you are lucky and God wills it, your spinal column and your brain will light up like the Fourth of July and you will get a taste of what it is like to be aware and functional on some sort of spiritual level.

You see, he got lucky and was semi-involuntarily catapulted to the exotic realms of Samadhi wherein his personal identity was negated and all he believed in dissolved and, with the help of some top dog dudes in one of the Tibetan Buddhist lineages, was able to come back and talk about it. He seems real happy about it too, smiling all the time, acting like he is glad to see everybody who shows up or drops by, emitting an air of confidence and self-assuredness that would be annoying if he were not so damn friendly. I mean he is beyond smug; he seems almost lost in his own little world which happens to actually be kind of huge. Like he takes this whole guru thing real seriously; like he can't find the zipper for the suit or something; like, you know, he is not kidding or practicing or pretending.

Everyone in the group seems to respect and revere him even though at the same time everybody likes to laugh, and appears to already know and like each other. But sometimes it seems like there is sort of an odd undercurrent, like everyone there just wants to be close to him and accepts the presence of all the others because there is no way around it. Like if they came and nobody else showed up it would be OK with them, maybe even kind of cool.

---

16 Kundalini is the dormant spiritual energy held at the base of the spine and awakened by shaktipat initiation.
17 The Sushumna is the primary nerve running from the base of the spine to the crown of the head, the possessor of all worlds, qualities, and universes.

And that is why I would like to lie to you and discourage you from coming. It is not that there has ever seemed to be too many people there or that his capacity has ever seemed even remotely exceeded or for that matter fully engaged; it's just that I, personally, don't like the idea of stumbling around in a huge sea of people clamoring to get a glance at what is going on. Selfish? Well, yes. Hung up on the material plane? I suppose. Contrary to what spiritual awareness is supposed to be all about? Hey, I am not the enlightened one...gimmee my Guru and screw all of you!

And, by the way, there are no beautiful women or handsome men there. No one has ever gotten lucky or formed a lasting relationship with someone they met there. Significant others don't even bother to show up and keep an eye on things. Everyone is so excessively spiritually oriented they seem more or less oblivious to each other. Occasionally a semi-attractive stranger does wander in, but they do not come back or bring friends or give out their phone number or anything. Frankly, the longer people attend the duller and more spaced out they seem to become; I mean what do you expect? They sit around in the dark with their eyes closed... ✺

Thank You

Mandy Hooper

A bright Light has been fixed in place over my life since I arrived at Hard Light. It is tangible; it is solid. Through the technique of the bellows breath and the gift of shaktipat, each day for me is a magical tuning progression. In essence, this is the most important place I have ever been.

I am in a place of acceptance here as I see the adorable ones gather. People who embrace the highest aspects of the Self. People who want to live from the inside out.

Mark is our Teacher

He has branded us with the name Shakti

He is our inner and outer teacher. He says remember to meditate every day. This becomes his access point within us. Since Mark gifted me with shaktipat, the energy changes and yet builds daily. It is a type of sifting and shifting. Shakti is very busy and says move out of the way, I have come. Shakti is dictatorial within me, yet gives me gifts I have not earned. A day of immersion in expanding love, a night of tears, revelations and forgiveness. A day of complete joy, a night of movement up and down my spine. And ribboned through each day and night is a High Voltage energy, buzzing. Mark's transmission has turned up the volume. As I watch the energy changing volumes within me, I can also see and feel the effects it has on others and situations around me.

I feel deeply protected by my teacher. And I know I can talk with him about anything. It is an extremely special feeling and you can see all here radiating a peaceful glow, as we are protected and enjoying the movement.

Patterns that I have struggled to change within me have suddenly and easily disappeared, only to be replaced with something more exciting. I am quieter now and can feel a deep stillness. I feel more and more grounded. I feel a sense of being connected to something Vast. I feel heat, where I once was so cold. I feel cushioned and my memory is clearer. And I feel the silent crackling live wire within me, ready to make its Mark.

I like this place in me. I am not rushing to find an answer anymore. One day I will breathe the Great Breath again. One day I shall go beyond that. I hope we all go there soon.

And it is Powerful to see Mark sitting in Hard Light

waiting

~ for Us ~

Om Nirvikalpa Samadhi

THE PRACTICE

Spiritual Practices: *Those activities, thoughts, and feelings that draw us closer to the highest reality.*

My Sitting Meditation

Anonymous

1. Dark blue mountain between my eyes.
2. Blood rushing up the body to the brain.
3. Sturdy hard metal penetrating through my spine.
4. A screw pointing toward me spinning between my eyebrows.
5. The heat and light from a flashlight just a few inches away from my face.
6. Being a tensed thread and a balloon simultaneously.
7. Muffled low-pitched drumming background.
8. Being in an elevator without walls and ceiling going up rapidly, and exploding with a sound of gunshot on my chest. Expanding with gentle heat, stillness and silence.
9. Two-inch diameter heavy iron pole through my chest between my lungs.

Sangha Populus Tremuloides

Barbara Jo Fleming

Tempest shivered aspens
whisper mantras *OM*.
Anchored *NA* in vast fecund
roots serpentine, communal,
ritually slurp liquid trinities *MA*.
Light, chlorophyll metabolizes *SHI* into
concentric rings that diminish
VA evermore towards heartwood.
Fall golden, doggedly returns.
Frost strips all naked.
Gnarled tributaries fracture
space *YA*. Undone
I, the path through disparate trunks
and forest chimera,
for silent footfall listen. *OM*

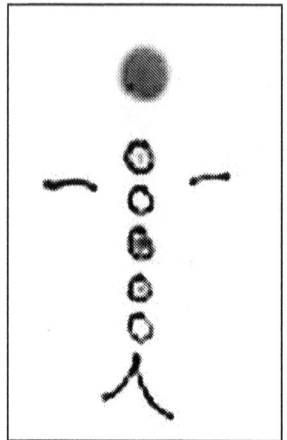

Namah Shivaya
Marcelle Marshall

Rising Sun

Barbara Hogan

Every day I open the gate to a beautiful garden. Hummingbird is here, Dove just landed and overhead crescent Moon. Coral clouds streak across the pale blue sky fading to yellow with the rising sun.

Minnie Mouse pops out of the rain gutter and scurries down the Oleander branch. The clouds are creamy now, the sky bluer. Two cawing Crows swoop over the canyon, Doves perching, Thrasher hopping closer to feeder, Towhees waiting their turn. The shrubs are squeaking and tweeting with Finches, Sparrows, Juncos and Warblers. Blue Jay and Thrasher breakfast together until crossing legs scare them off, creating an opening for Hummer to sip from blooming Hesperaloe. Towhee snags a few seeds while Thrasher gargles at the water basin.

Pearl white light frosts the mountain ridges; a sprinkler whirrs on wetting the parched hillside, cars head up Saddle Peak. The Sun pops over the ridge and the smaller birds emerge from the shrubs and perch on the branch tips of the dying tree signaling me to wind down the mountain.

Pushing open the tall wooden gate, pausing to look at the tall, arching Cane Begonias, dangling Apricot Abutilon bells, glad to see that Dipladenia has wound its way through Melaleuca and opened a big white yellow-centered trumpet. Walking past maiden hair Fern and golden Acorus, I push open another wooden gate and walk under the arching Melaleuca and past the salt and wind and full-sun-hardy potted plants and step up to the deck leading to the destination, an earthly frontier, as far as the eye can see; the expansive ocean, shimmering, glistening fluid light. Om Na Ma Shivaya, Om Na Ma Shivaya, Om Na Ma Shivaya, I retrace my steps, Om Na Ma Shivaya, pruning, Om Na Ma Shivaya, deadheading, Om Na Ma Shivaya, feeding, Om Na Ma Shivaya, watering, Om Na Ma Shivaya, breathing, Om Na Ma Shivaya........ ○

crashcourse

Virginia LeRossignol Blades

i. first thursdays

The regal tree at Aldersgate
is a calming tree.
Her vast crown sweeping up
and tangly magnolia fingers
spilling down
in reassurance

I hail her now,
seeking console
before rounding the corner toward
Darshan
this word that tumbles clumsy in my mouth
like foreign spices
or unpolished hot stones

Now at the brink of the hall
feet stutter at the threshold
feigned composure parting to reveal
the well-worn buzz
intended for fleeing predators
or lifting vehicles off trapped children
not sitting quietly with strangers
in a darkened room
circling an Enigma

No escape
from the Gaze

Then there's Lee—
her bright greeting like a snug orange life-vest
i'm suited up for my trip with a comforting pat
then gently aimed toward
the opening
and the next incessant barrage
of internal chatter:

where to sit,
greet, not greet?
where to look,
meet the gaze?
smile, not smile?
curtsy? bow?
what is expected in
this beckoning universe?

gawky debutante
stumbling on her quickened pride
reflexes bracing against
Authority

i flicker between
veneration & conceit
avoid, deflect
frantic testing of shields
    rendered useless
until
the room careens
gravity alters for a heartbeat
    where is North?
the needle spins wildly
shuddering toward dark places
Please don't make me look!
but the gaze, the gaze
no hiding behind eyelids!
such noise in here how
do i act, who is acting
just be yourself.
but who is that?
me me ME

a spooked creature
tethered, yet led willingly
lovingly
to be shredded and
devoured

ii. first intensive

The night before my first malibu intensive
i dreamt of
a cliff swathed in fog
    a crunching gravel path & a hillside temple
      a sensei & the challenge:
        to rappel blindly down the shrouded precipice
          into unknown territory
            where the rest of the mission would be revealed
some sort of crashcourse

but i don't know this ninja stuff!
what am i doing on this clifftop?
unskilled, unprepared
not even packing a toothbrush!
And anyway,
even if i DID enlist somehow
    though i can't recall
why would i step up to a mission
without being able to scope the terrain?
how tactical is THAT?
within that sea of shielding fog
there might be jaggy rocks
    or a bottomless sea
      or worse yet, monsters!
I don't want to die

But the dream is clear:
it's not the results, but the intent.
The sensei means no harm
it's only a lively game to be played out
    never mind the stakes
    or this body so readily broken
Thanks for showing up.
Here's the rope. Ready, Go!

Now creeping up an unfamiliar canyon road in a rare summer fog
Last night's dream is summoned forth
glimmering on the moist windshield
thick mists cloak the aching sky
with an infinite whiteness
until there is no outer or inner
no thing
but the bubble
and the movement
toward the destination
last night's dream & this day merging
into one
tonal moment

am i headed toward a cliff?
will there be monsters?
a rope?
i can't   i can't
this fog conceals the handholds!
what happens if you fall?
        frantic clinging
to the road curving through the white envelope

i spot the sign DRESSER,
veer cautiously from pavement onto a gravel path
tip over the lip into this vast milky bowl
crunching tires the only sense holding back freefall
reach bottom, park
exit my bubble refuge
stumble up the veiled footpath,
elbows knocking the rearview mirrors of cars clustered with their fenders
all pointing toward the portal
        & the Guru within

the dream unravels in long skeins
But it's NOT a temple on a cliff!!
No mission, no ninjas... See?
Just a little wooden house perched there
        like a frosted apparition

           in an odd summer fog
clinging to the membrane that holds it all back
logic collapses
human reason ransacked
trying to obliterate the dream
which was then
is now
taking form on this foggy cliff top
with such inevitability

Change course before its too late!

But then there's Lee, gleaming
as she sits at her wobbly cardtable,
life-vest outstretched.
            Thanks for coming,
            take your shoes off
            the Guru is inside.
            Ready, Go!

Don't fixate on the stakes.
We're just inside a cloud.
The sun will burn it away
in time
Besides, He means us no harm,
the shredding
            the devouring.
It's nothing personal.
Trust this.
Just another afternoon
in the hard light. ✿

Sitting still

Jason Handler

Simply sitting still
Sounds so easy
But i'll tell you why
I like to kiss the feet of my guru.
There's a channel that runs
From the corner of the big toe
All the way up through the crown.
A straight shot.
You can only see in stillness.

Simply sitting still
Sounds so easy
But i'll tell you why my guru said,
"Silence is the greatest teacher
Because it rewards those who listen carefully."
And it's true,
Music is a perfect reflection of life
And it's heard through the space
In between the notes.

Simply sitting still
Sounds so easy
But i'll tell you what…
Those who know
Movement is much easier.
Appreciate
The work it takes to find the silence
that comes from
simply sitting still. ✪

Rising Sun: Spiritual Masters and the Art of Meditation

Alyson Dutch

A Behind the Scenes Look at a Meditation Retreat on Ojai's Auspicious Sulphur Mountain

Past the sleepy, four mile square town of Santa Paula, past one of America's original oil wells and up a one-lane road on Sulphur Mountain, sits a place called Meher Mount. Many years ago, on this piece of land, a woman named Agnes Baron hosted the most revered and highest spiritual superstar of India—a man named Meher Baba. The land has since borne his name and serves as an ecumenical retreat center. Although one of eight retreat centers in Ojai and many around the world, this place is no ordinary Kumbaya weekend campsite. Those of the spiritual persuasion will describe this place as one of the most auspicious in North America. It is just this quality that attracted one of America's spiritual superstars here to host his annual summer retreat. Mark Griffin is the protégé of a similarly revered and famous yogi named Muktananda. Griffin and Muktananda are part of what is called the "Siddha lineage."

Beginning on the day of the solstice (the longest day of the year, and before organized religion, the highest holy day of the year), Griffin arrived with forty devotees, mostly from Southern California and some from as far away as Seattle, San Francisco, and New Mexico. The group erected a 30' x 60' tent on the open land overlooking the hills of Ojai (complete with an outdoor kitchen including refrigerators) and entered into a seventy-two-hour meditation retreat.

"The air is thin here," (even though the physical location of the land is maybe 500 feet above sea level) Griffin says during a Thursday night orientation lit by only a single candle. Griffin is surrounded by cross-legged meditators sitting in the flaxen mowed grass, some in lawn chairs. He further explains that Meher Mount is a place where enlightenment can happen—and because the "fabric is worn thin" here, it is more probable that the divine spark within any of us could finally permeate our physical body and mind to shuttle us off to the Hindu version of "heaven" and perhaps to the level of enlightenment where he lives.

While taking a tour of Meher Mount's library, one learns that Meher Baba (born: 25 February 1894) was the Hindu "avatar" of our age. The text on a wall that describes his life uses a capital "H" when referring to "Him" and equates his spiritual maturation to that of Jesus, Mohammed and Buddha. When I asked one of the retreatants about Baba (or "Father"), she tipped her straw hat with a brooch featuring "His" photo on the ribbon. The gal, an executive from LA's highest-ranking entertainment law firm who drove her Porsche to Meher Mount says, "Baba was known as a literal incarnation of God."

Interestingly enough, Mark Griffin, founder of a meditation organization in Los Angeles, San Francisco, Seattle and New Mexico is not considered an Avatar, but has achieved a very high level of enlightenment, known as "samadhi." In LA, where many fancy themselves as a guru of this or that, Griffin is said to be the "real thing." Griffin studied with Bhagavan Muktananda until Muktananda's Mahasamadhi (passing) in 1982. Griffin excelled so quickly that he became one of a few Americans to carry on the tradition of shaktipat (igniting the divine spark within). The rigorous training that Griffin went through with his teacher far surpasses the eleven hours a day of meditation that this group will endure over the weekend.

Griffin's Hard Light Meditation Center has a small, but very devoted group of fifty to seventy-five students. "One of the reasons that I love Mark," said the owner of a PR firm in LA, "is that he gives a sort of fast track to enlightenment." Although it might seem fitting to say that an American dreamt up such a concept, it was actually the basis of Muktananada's work and very unusual for an Indian spiritual teacher. "Traditionally, the teacher and student work together for many, many years," said a close student of Griffin's and an avid spiritual academic. "Often, a student will be imbued with 'shaktipat' which is sort of like an energetic blessing that opens the right channels of the student's mind to receive and experience an automatic enlightenment." Whether the student can actually realize it and use it in this life is where the training comes in. Working with Griffin, students learn how to recognize and "burn off" karma. When our karma is finally exhausted, enlightenment occurs. Similar to the Catholic rite of confession which ritualistically wipes the slate clean for awhile to receive the full blessing of God, the Hindus believe that karma must be burned off—to jump to the next level. In Catholic-ese, this is similar to the concept of everlasting life or heaven.

That evening at the orientation, the land's caretakers warn of rattlesnakes and urge that retreatants use their flashlights to avoid turning their ankles in gopher holes. They end on a note that sends a silent grumble through the crowd when they ask that the tents that were pitched under the 500-year-old "Meher Baba Tree" be moved. The property withstood a fire in 1985, which burned down the house and other trees, but saved a gargantuan oak, that shelters a memorial to Baba and to Agnes Baron. Though the property has been rented by Hard Light for four days, tourists continue to visit Meher Mount to see the Baba Tree and might find an encampment under it tantamount to a tent city in the Taj Mahal.

As the weekend progresses, the group "sits" with Griffin from 5-6 a.m. 9-11, 2:30–6:30 and again from 8:30–10:00. It is indeed a meditation marathon. Some wiggle and look for their water bottles every twenty minutes, other more seasoned meditators sit blissfully, soaking up the "transmissions" that Griffin provides silently.

Griffin, a large 50-year old man with a long curly ponytail, sits at the front of the tent in what seems an active trance. He prays silently, but his lips move unintelligibly. In the a.m., he launches into a fascinating dissertation that explains the dissonance between being human and being enlightened. He describes in utter, complicated detail how the "ocean of consciousness" (or God in Christian-ese) lives in a body and how it is activated through meditation. He instructs how to meditate to achieve this purpose. As the "guru" it is his job to help each student along by energetically showing them the way. It's sort of like a spiritual yellow brick road, but the man behind the curtain is NOT an imposter.

With the recent proliferation of adventure travel, a meditation retreat such as this certainly qualifies. Hard Light holds these retreats each summer at various retreat centers—this year it was Meher Mount. In years past it was held in the High Sierras or Santa Cruz.

Though the retreatants are supposed to remain silent, there are many interesting conversations throughout the weekend that center around Griffin's two-hour discourse about a deity named "Devi," and the personification of her ten arms, each of which is a goddess in her own right. After the teaching, an extemporaneous half-hour pause and a forty-minute meditation, the group plays "follow the leader" on a walking meditation. At dinner over stuffed bell peppers, baked tofu and bruschetta, the conversation finally turns to bursts of laughter over the retreatants' former high school incarnations.

All in all, spending 12-14 hours a day "contemplating your belly button" as Archie Bunker would have described it is no easy task. Each participant, no matter how seasoned a meditator, struggles with bad cases of "monkey mind" and some admit that they don't want to become enlightened. Two women (one an author on the subject and the other a Ph.D. of organizational development) are heard sharing that they "simply want to learn to live this life more mindfully and richly—forget the enlightenment!" as they roll their eyes knowing that it would be too difficult to attain this.

In between teachings, Griffin holds question and answer sessions in the tent—or "hall" as the structure is referred to. Called "satsang," the students ask personal questions about how they see their lives coming together or in many cases seeming to fall apart. "A spiritual life reveals to us the cycles of the Samskaric circle," says Griffin with a knowing nod and growing smile of understanding. The group joins Griffin in affirming they all can relate to the question and everyone laughs together. Griffin goes on to explain that this "falling apart" is really a "purification" and a necessary experience for every human to experience in their average 84,000 incarnations before reaching enlightenment.

After each session, the group circles the tent in a single-file line three times and upon returning, does the same thing. The movement signifies keeping a "warmth" or strength of energetic intention around this temporary place of teaching. Most walk silently, anxious to get to the next meal, and some talk. Two women discuss the seeming infinite amount of names that Griffin imparts about every state of being and amazing quantification the Hindus seem to have figured. "Sometimes I just sit there and think to myself that he just makes this all up," says one pixie blond. "How the heck does he come up with numbers like 84,000 lives before we become enlightened?!" The other more seasoned redhead explains that from her studies in India that many of the teachers spend so much time studying meditation and the process of enlightenment that they almost have nothing else to do, so of course, they come up with names for everything. The blonde responds that the organized large religions of the world must have done everything they could to "dumb this down" and simplify, thus introducing just ONE major prophet and only twelve disciples, for example. "That could be true," the redhead says as they head toward the lunch tent.

What does it take to put something like this together? High on meditation, low on activity, a Hard Light retreat does not include any ropes classes, trust falls or the like. It requires a high degree of patient focus and the ability to sit still. With much more ritual than a Catholic Mass on Christmas Day, the Hard Light prep team first erects the tent and stations a chair, rug, table, flowers and decorative fabric hangings of various spiritual significance throughout the tent. Griffin sits at the front. A "puja table" stands opposite Griffin at the back of the tent. Forty pounds of rice, enough saffron to choke a horse, endless sticks of incense, (this batch that reminds me of the shampoo I used as a kid), candles, and frankincense are amongst some of the buckets of ritual tools used in plenty. A very staining red powder (traditional Indian kum-kum) is used to dot the forehead of each retreatant every morning. Lots of coconuts are also used.

Every morning, Griffin says prayers over the puja table, which has been topped with a copper bowl and tied with significantly colored threads. Two 20-pound bags of rice are poured over the bowl. The rice is a symbol of life. A coconut is placed atop the rice mound and Griffin dips his finger into the red powder and imprints a red dot, similar to what one would see on a married Indian woman's forehead, onto the coconut. Flowers flank the puja table; rose water is splashed into the offering. The significance of this table is not to worship the coconut or befriend it as Tom Hanks did of his coconut in the film "Cast Away," but it serves as a symbol of the group honoring the Infinite Divine, or "Ishvara"[18] as seen through these chosen elements of foodstuffs. Griffin then goes through the tent applying a red dot on all the participants' foreheads. The dots symbolize the Divine connection of all the retreatants who are here to focus on God and how it shows up in them for the next three days. Griffin returns to his chair and applies a dot to his forehead as well.

---

18 Ishvara is the lord and ruler over all, the Supreme being.

And so it goes for three days. On Sunday night, Griffin explains that the retreat is drawing to a close and that tomorrow morning, he will be giving final blessings and helping each student to "close themselves up" so they can "reenter the world." He does this silently and through a beautiful ritual where he invites each student up to the front of the tent and gives them a mango and t-shirt with an "Om symbol" on the front. The t-shirt is symbolic of the retreat where the focus was on what is called "the Om point." The Om point is the place between the absolute nature of God and what Griffin describes as the "throb of creation" or Ishvara.

After this weekend it becomes obvious that this tradition does not subscribe to the Adam and Eve and seven-day creation theory.

The retreatants share breakfast and then begin to pack up their tents and pack their cars. The large tent is dissembled and all the giant woks, refrigerators and kitchen tools are packed into trucks.

As I leave, I take care to remain grounded and focus on driving. Last time I left this retreat, I felt like Johnny Depp in "Fear & Loathing in Las Vegas" and really had a difficult time doing more than one thing at a time. I think that I insisted on talking to my boyfriend on my cell phone all the way home on the five-hour drive from Santa Cruz. This time, I stop at a ranch on the way out of Ojai to pick up a brown bag of freshly picked apricots on the side of the road. Each bag is marked with "$3" on the side; I pick the most fragrant and leave a $5 dollar bill. I don't have the change and don't care. I'm happy to be on my way home and hear the radio again, yet I find myself yearning for the protection and incredible peace I felt while in retreat. As I descend into the Santa Paula valley and pass that old oil well, I feel like I've slipped out of a womb. I feel warm, peaceful and satiated. I dare to check my voicemail and begin to rearrange my attention to focus on clients who have called over the weekend and my boyfriend who is waiting to meet me for dinner. And so it goes, until next summer, when I will do it all over again. ☉

Electronic Conversations

Bob Schulenburg

Meditation without Mark

Tuesday night, for some undisclosed reason, Mark did not physically attend the group meeting up on the hill in Malibu. The next day I sent him a little letter. Here it is with an interesting reply from him, especially inasmuch as I was not expecting one...

From: Bob
To: Mark
Sent: 12/19/2005
Subject: Meditation without you

Last night was very cool; everyone is so well "trained" they just sat down and went about their meditative business. Now, I could not tell you exactly what any of them were up to but I was very impressed by their self-reliance, calmness, and intensity of focus, like they are gonna do it with you or without you, which of course is a relativistic proposition since you were no doubt "with us." Still, it was nice to get a sense that each one of them could do what they needed to do and have a satisfying worthwhile experience. It caused me to reflect into the future when each one will be a competent teacher in their own right, not in this lifetime of course...

See you Thursday,
Bob

From: Mark
To: Bob
Sent: 12/19/2005
Subject: Re: Meditation without you

Bob
You have glimpsed a secret.
You are going to bend time and space
as the future unfolds.

Love, Mark

Mahasamadhi

From: Dan
To: Bob
Sent: 09/25/2005
Subject: Mahasamadhi

Well, Bob, I see that Mark's next intensive is called "Mahasamadhi," a word generally synonymous with DEATH. A two-day intensive...I guess it is going to be a SLOW death. Well, it's been nice knowing you...

From: Bob
To: Dan
Sent: 09/25/2005
Subject: Mahasamadhi

Silly Earth Man! The event is in honor of Muktananda's release/escape from the bodily dimension of the Guru-Game. So far as I know, Mark has no intention of killing any of us. Please cancel the séance. I do not believe it will be necessary and forget any thoughts of offing yourself to join the party. (Do psychically tune in; we will be expecting you.)

Had you heard? A group of magicians intent on protecting us from the hurricanes performed some rituals and discovered the only accessible demons of sufficient stature to contend with the storms were employed by the US government.

~~~~

Shakti

From: Bob
To: Mark
Sent: 12/20/2005
Subject: She

Hi Mark, during the first session of the intensive last week I had a very wonderful experience. I tried to put it more or less into words even though there is no way...

What happened to me Saturday was so powerful, so intimate, so amazing, it was like layer after layer of subtle Divine yin-yang energies emerged, interwove, nestled into each other, expanded and kept on expanding. There was a huge presence emanating from her that invited and invoked and involved levels of myself I ordinarily never even get to be conscious of. We merged together into this amazing geometric form, alive, pulsating and it just kept growing...it seemed like wherever I went she was already there, radiant and provocative. The whole time I felt as if I were with my dearest friend, like two little kids off on some mind-boggling adventure, secure and inspired because they were together. Nothing in my previous experience or ability to imagine ever hinted at the richness and depth and sense of union manifest in those moments; my entire being was captivated and consumed and costumed in splendor. It was as if she were a channel of a cosmic flow of unlimited proportions; the more I became enraptured in it the more it would manifest and entice me into going beyond with her, so deliciously, sensuously, softly, secretly with her...

So, anyway, in your opinion, does it sound like it would be safe to say I am talking about Shakti here? I figure it is either that or I am completely deluded and should consider getting professional help...

Love,
Bob

At this point Bob wandered off babbling incoherently, smiling like a shark who just won a seal lottery, gesturing in the air to imaginary friends and inviting them all to come with him. He apparently no longer recognizes time or space in the conventional sense and thinks everything is wonderful. Attempts to apprehend the woman responsible were abandoned when it became decisively evident she is not from this realm and only plays with this reality in manners and on occasions when it suits or amuses her. ✪

Meditation Intensive

Kai Markowitz

August, 2004
Santa Monica Mountains, California

I breathe in and I breathe out. I breathe in and I breathe out. Just a few minutes into a day-long meditation and already I can feel the heat rising, my skin beginning to tingle, my body growing dense as the energy begins to accumulate. The leading edge of all the long meditations—clearing of obstacles—is underway, the removal of that which prevents you from experiencing yourself as you truly are.

> There are only questions. Why do people get involved with meditation, with the study of Enlightenment? What is it that drives someone to investigate what's inside themselves, to try and discover who and what they truly are?

The pressure begins to pull in towards my spine, and there is the clear sensation of a post extending through the middle of my body. I hear the woman behind me breathing; her breath is ragged and she is sniffling. I begin to feel anger rising from within. I want to turn around and tell her to cut it the fuck out. Then everything will be OK, I'll feel better. My spine is hard, like a piece of rebar. The pressure in my body continues to increase. Discomfort on all sides. It's unbearable.

> How do we define the value of a person? What is it that makes a person what they are? How do we define ourselves to ourselves? As time passes, and the illusions of youth, beauty, fame, and fortune fade away, what's left? Will any of these things remain? As we skate off the edge of the social spectrum and become invisible to the culture in which we live, how will we define ourselves?

Razor blades drag across every nerve. I want to get up and scream, to hit things, break things. I can't stand it anymore. The pressure is everywhere; muscles contracting from the energy, my body has become rigid. Like one long isometric exercise from Hell that will never end. And then my body begins to shake. There's a pop in my ears. I hear something that has no sound. My head involuntarily turns to the right and I stare out the window over the mountaintop's horizon and out into the Pacific Ocean. Something's coming. I see it but it cannot be seen.

Sarada Devi was the consort of Sri Ramakrishna, a well-known Indian guru of the 19th century. I recently saw a series of photos of Sarada Devi taken over the span of a decade, from her early forties to her early fifties; the series of photos struck me as being a beautiful pictorial describing the phases of the process of Enlightenment. In the first picture she sits cross-legged on the floor, radiant, still possessing the beauty of her youth, with a beatific expression of tranquility, and a self-possessed look that says "I am." In the second picture from a few years later, a much plainer woman sits cross-legged on the floor and stares into the camera. Her age now clearly beginning to show, it is a picture of transition. Her eyes have taken on an expression of emptiness and an edge of bafflement. I can hear the words in her head, "I don't understand any of this, where will this take me?" The questions have begun to overwhelm the answers. The next picture comes from a few years later. A clearly middle-aged woman sits on what may be a bench, hands upturned on her lap, eyes gazing off and down to the side. She looks wild. Her personal identity having finally been annihilated by what she truly is, the energy streams off of her like fire.

Everything stops. Completely still. The mind stops. The physical pressure evaporates swiftly, radiating from the body in pulses of joy. I know that it is love that defines what a human being is, being the energy that binds the complex human form together. I know that everything I ever thought I was is nothing more than a complex weave of desire accumulated over time immemorial, and that this fabric has obscured what I truly am. I am the path, I am its goal. I am awakened. Wave after wave of awareness arises within me, the knowledge arising unbidden, instantaneously. I have the answer to questions that I never knew existed before this moment. What was absent suddenly presents itself. Like having a chip plugged into your head—"I know kung fu."

It's the last night of a five-day meditation on the banks of the Ganges in India. Shivaratri. Dawn approaches. I've been sitting in meditation for six hours. I can't remember when it started or when it will end. Again and again I experience the dissolution of personal identity, thought shutting down as universal consciousness arises. Complete freedom. Every part of my body is totally aware and totally captivated by the experience of the moment, held perfectly upright by the energy coursing through my spine. And again and again I feel myself reassembling under the weight of the fabric of the desire that binds my personal identity into place. First I feel it coming, then edges of the fabric begin to engulf me, and finally everything closes down. I feel trapped, claustrophobic. It's like being in prison. The teaching is pointed and clear.

After close to nine hours, the Meditation Intensive is coming to an end. After moving at the speed of light without any motion for the entire day, I begin to feel myself skim the atmosphere as I descend to the plane of mundane consciousness once again. I'm exhausted. Music is playing, some kind of Buddhist chant. It reminds me that there was a time when I felt that enlightenment was to be found somewhere else, perhaps in the East. Now the music just sounds empty. What will the process of enlightenment look like in the West? Me. I am the face of awakening in the West.

The only person I've ever heard describe what it feels like to shift from the ecstasy of universal consciousness back into the world of mundane reality was a vampire slayer. And what she said goes something like this:

"Wherever I was I was happy, at peace. I knew that everyone I cared about was all right. Time didn't mean anything. Nothing had form but I was still me. And I was warm and I was loved and I was finished. Complete. I don't understand about theology or dimensions, or any of it really, but I think I was in heaven. And now I'm not. I was torn out of there. Pulled out. Everything here is hard, and bright, and violent. Everything I feel, everything I touch, this is Hell."

On the floor of Enlightenment.
Demons, be gone.
Friends and family, be gone.
Mind's precious ideas, be gone.
In the Ocean, only water.
In the Ocean, only the taste of Enlightenment.

All blessings to God.
All blessings to the Guru.
All blessings to the Self.
May this hall be auspicious for everyone.
May my sadhana be auspicious for everyone.
May my practice bear fruit and free me from
this endless wheel of sorrow.
May all awaken.

✽

Totems

Brian Hughes

The rattlesnake
Taught me how to swallow my own tale
The wolf
Taught me how to eat and run
The sparrow
Taught me how to sing from my heart
The pig
Taught me how to speak what is True
Coyote
Taught me the value of staying lean
Fox:
"Just shut up and listen"
Badger:
"Learn to kick some ass, white boy"
Tadpole:
"Patience"
Frog:
"Learn to blend"
Dog:
"And I will always love you"
God:
"All thee above"

Empty Vessel

Wanda Rhodes

When I meditate,
I remember who I am
while the world forgets.

THE EXPERIENCE

The Experience: *Everyone has his or her own version of a spiritual experience. For some, it's in daily life; for others it's in meditation. And for others at certain times, it's the absence of any discernable experience at all.*

The Lemmings

Rudrakshananda

scamper... scamper... scurry... scurry... scamper... scamper
scurry... scurry... scamper... scamper... scurry... scurry
scamper... scamper... snack... scurry... scurry
scurry... scurry... yawn... scamper... scamper
scamper... sleep... scamper
scurry... nap... scurry

SHAKTIPAT!

scurry
scamper
scurryscamper
scamperscamperscurryscurry
scurryscurryscamperscamperscurryscurryscamperscamper
scamperscamperscurryscurryscamperscamperscurryscurryscamper
scurryscurryscamperscamperscurryscurryscamperscamperscurry
scamperscamperscurryscurryscamperscamperscurryscurryscamper
scurryscurryscamperscamperscurryscurryscamperscamperscurry

REALIZATION!

panicfleerundenypanicfleerundenypanicfleerundenypanicfleerun
deny
fleerundenypanicfleerundenypanicfleerundenypanicfleerundeny
panic
rundenypanicfleerundenypanicfleerundenypanicfleerundenypanic
flee
denypanicfleerundenypanicfleerundenypanicfleerundenypanicflee
run

W
H
E
E
E
!
!
!

splash

Gracewaves

Paige Hetherington

With each visit to the ocean, surfing provides a remarkably different experience. The shades of sky are never the same. The light and colors are always in motion. The movement of energy through the water manifests unique patterns and the swell direction, tides, and wind vary with each session. The groundswells of Prakriti[19] and the wind swells of Purush[20] travel huge distances before reaching our shore. Although a surfer's selfish drive to be in position to capture this energy may pervade the mind, the heart still swells upon witnessing a fellow surfer's stoke. When the elements come together perfectly, long rides invoke an exciting newness which lights up uncharted areas of the brain. At times, the excitement is greater than the mind's ability to assemble and it may not be possible to clearly remember the ride.

The ocean reminds us we are not alone and surfacing emotions are countless. Sharks stir fears, likely elsewhere when dolphins reveal their proximity. They play and protect, sharing waves and uplifting dispositions. When it is glassy and clear, darting rays and other creatures are visible below.

The ocean humbles the bold as well as the timid. Sometimes the waves simply crush and promise the experience of being held down with expended breath and surrounding blackness. When relaxed, a thrashing spin cycle conjures a Siddha's whisper and the will to surface arises.

In 1978, the movie *Big Wednesday* was released depicting the lives of California surfers from the early sixties into the seventies. On the winter solstice this year, Big Wednesday manifested itself in Southern California. Waves reaching heights greater than twenty feet graced our beaches. I paddled out knowing I could not surf such size. Watching some of the best, non-contest surfing I had seen first hand I felt exhilarated. Mark says if you want to learn how to do something you should practice and hang around those who are adept. If I stay committed to surfing for ten or twenty years, I may become a pretty decent surfer. Maybe even good enough to ride big waves. Maybe not. Even so, I can tell it will be worth it: wetsuits, cold water, impatience, wipeouts, injuries, crowds, etc.

---

19 Prakriti is the principle of manifest creation, nature itself.
20 Purush is the individual soul; the in-dwelling form of God as the individual soul.

The same holds true for meditation with Mark. My experience studying with him has been very similar to my hours logged in the water; sitting, waiting, watching for opportunities to move beyond the matrix of time. I remember him talking once and describing the waves of patience, compassion, kindness and love as waves that go on forever. Like being alive and simultaneously unplugged, surfing and meditation have presented moments which demonstrate an ultimate freedom.

Mark is a surfer of gracewaves, stringing those moments together and magnetizing a liberated state. His presence is the example, infinitely more valuable than a few moments while surfing. Surfing may bring glimpses of freedom but Mark shows how to dwell therein. ✪

The Wave
Marcelle Marshall

The names i'll call her

Jason Handler

Nectar
That's what i'll call her
Because she tastes like the sweetness of the sun
Filtered through the fruit on every tree

Shakti
That's what i'll call her
Because
I can feel my insides tremble
As she dances in between heaven and earth

Grace
That's what i'll call her
Because
Our experience together is a boon sent from above.

❂

Old Song

Linda Horan

Today again as oft before
her vital touch bestowed
a joinder of divergent selves
a confluence of roads.
It had been my want of Other
that propelled me through the maze
a panicked craze
feverish daze
spent aching for relation
fusion.
And all of this was seen by her whose inner gaze forebode
the anguish of such searing pain in my struggle to withhold
her stuff
her core
her essence
which I hated
which I craved
her knowledge of that single pulse
that solitary game of her body in a mirror playing lovers.
But I could not keep my bearings
as she ebbed and flowed through me
and ministered to grievous wounds brought on by fantasies
of a separate condition.
So I scaled the wall I'd molded of the dross of certainty
of poverty
satiety
all notions of our distance.
And in honor of my vantage
to this puerile mind she showed
the endlessness
unbounded bliss
expanse of Mother's Lode.

The Tale of the Siddha

Bob Schulenburg

One evening Mark told us a story about a very advanced Siddha who came across the body of a shepherd lying dead in the middle of his confused and agitated flock. The siddha entered into the body and began herding the sheep back to the man's home in the village where he had lived. He stayed in the body living the life of the shepherd; however the man's wife and all of the villagers could not help but notice something was dramatically different. He looked like the same man but there was indeed a very different level of being emanating from him.

Mark told us this story to illustrate a variety of aspects and considerations relative to ourselves, our lives, our bodies and our futures.

Later that night I wrote the following text and sent it to him.

The Rest of the Story:

The body of the now relocated Siddha lay in the field until a lost beggar happened across it. Unfortunately, he was standing next to it when two women from a nearby village passed by and hysterically ran and summoned a policeman. The beggar was arrested, charged with murder, and locked up to await trial.

That night he had a vivid dream in which one of the sheep stepped out of the herd and approached him. The sheep told him she knew the man did not kill the Siddha and it was through the Siddha's great love and spiritual power she was able to speak to him. She told him to bring the judge to her and she would tell him.

The judge, of course, was very skeptical yet decided inasmuch as the dead man was known to be a powerful and devout renunciate the court would go to the field with the beggar.

When they arrived and the beggar saw the many, many sheep all bunched together, his heart sank. How would he ever know which was the one? Then, miraculously, one came forward. The beggar recognized her and smiled and pointed her out to the judge. He walked over, giving thanks and blessings, and asked the sheep to please tell the judge what she had told him the night before. The sheep turned and faced the judge, opened her mouth and said "BAAAAAA."

They took the beggar away and hung him that very afternoon.

A powerful Siddha sat on a nearby hill and watched. As they were taking down the man's lifeless body, the Siddha considered entering into it thinking if he reanimated the body he could show the man had been telling the truth. Just as he was about to transfer his soul, a cow walked up to him and said. "Forget it, pal; this thing has already gotten way too complicated." The Siddha laughed and said, "You are right, let's go have a beer," and the two of them leisurely walked down the hill into town.

Mark wrote back to me:

That is exactly what happened! ✪

The moment we touched

Jason Handler

Who's in there she asked
As the elevator door shut
And I remember wondering the same thing
Curious for a way to call home
A way to ask
Where have you been?
A way to understand why
We quicken the blood
With things like chocolate and red wine
So that our hearts may beat faster and with that sense of synchronicity
We knew the moment we touched.

Emptiness, Wrathful Annihilation of Identity

Siddha Student

My compulsions as a sensory driven being are being obliterated by the force of the kundalini which has the binding power of time. The base and crown of my spine have been awakened and flooded with Divine Shakti which purifies my nadis, chakras, Ida, Pingala, and most importantly the Sushumna.[21]

Purification unlocks the strangle hold that the karmic data holds in my subtle body. I am no longer solely an experiencer of the senses being driven from one desire to the next. By redirecting the flow of the Prana away from the nine gates[22] and the left and right channel to the central channel. I awaken Sahasrara[23] which is the direct interface between God and man.

I know myself to be more than this body, mind, and energy. My identity reaches far beyond time and space. This is all possible by the Grace of God and the Guru manifestation.

THIS is all inherent in my design. Extinguishing my identity and merging with Ishvara, God's will, is my destiny.

Traveling the pole of opposites, illuminating sushumna and merging Infinite Consciousness and Infinite Unconsciousness and realizing both as empty is my aim.

Freedom to those who seek the Self!

Victory to all Gurus!

---

21 The Ida and Pingala are two main nadis of the spinal column in the subtle body and are located on the left and right sides of the central nerve, the Sushumna.

22 The nine gates refer to the nine openings in the body.

23 The Sahasrara is the chakra located at the crown of the head.

The Five Phases

Anonymous

FIRE
Inspiring.
like the unity
between
community and passion,
compassion
is the thread
that wakes the heart and mind.

EARTH
Generous
like the floor's
support
we constantly ignore.

METAL
In the time it would take
to refine a tropical beach
into
an iridescent pearl
I appreciate the subtlety of your nothings.

WATER
When you make like a jellyfish
Rhythm don't mean nothing.

WOOD
Generation
like a seated meditation
indivisible separation
the seeds of preparation
secure
knowing we're temporary
at
our destination.

THAT'S NOT MINE!

Camille Harris

"Prepare your seat." Mark has uttered those words countless times before but on this night something was different. As I prepared to meditate, I suddenly became frightened. I looked around the room and the once vibrant colors were now opaque, and the rich texture and dimension of the space suddenly became two-dimensional. I felt distant from my once vital body and my chest began to tighten. What was this? How could I have gotten to this place? As a child I was known as the "mild one," never quick to anger, always observing.

And there I sat, far removed from my known persona. How could I forgive her for treating me that way, I didn't deserve that! To be left, betrayed, shut out. The anger again began to rise. "This was not mine," I thought. "No, no, this was her anger projecting onto me." Anger didn't belong to me. I could observe it, judge it, but it never came anywhere near me. It was out there, something others dealt with. I observed anger from a distance, a voyeur, never really understanding the gift behind the unlikable wrapping paper. Like the time I observed a couple arguing across the street. Shaking my head thinking, "What a waste of time." And I've never really understood the frustrated shopper in the checkout line or the driver that would proudly display a hand gesture as he passed me by on the freeway. What a waste of time; to be so frustrated, unconnected, and ANGRY.

Well, there I was preparing to sit and meditate on compassion, on a day that marked a shift in global consciousness. There I sat, frightened and ANGRY. This doesn't belong to me!!! All the while not knowing if I was going to return from this place. And as we began, I prayed. I prayed and surrendered to the moment. It was all that I could do. I didn't want to stay suspended here. "Please show me, show me what I'm not able to see." And I sat, trying to give rise to love, to bodhicitta.[24] And I prayed, "Please show me." "Keep breathing," I told myself, "you'll be fine, just keep breathing. Give rise to bodhicitta." My heart was still closed off. I was still ANGRY.

And then something hit me like a tidal wave. I was back in my childhood standing in front of my dresser placing a note in the top drawer

---

[24] Bodhicitta is the ideal of enlightenment and the burning love of that enlightenment.

wondering if they would see it. "I AM RUNNING AWAY BECAUSE I DON'T FEEL LIKE I BELONG HERE." And as I moved through my life I began to reflect on all the times I felt unloved, not seen, not heard and discounted. I began to cry; I began to cry for that little innocent girl, that awkward teenager, and that confused adult. I couldn't stop crying. The feeling overwhelmed me. Yet in that very same moment of despair, I understood. I understood my anger. I understood its source, its root. The tears kept flowing, I began to soften, and the tightness in my chest began to subside. And as my breath began to deepen, my anger towards her subsided. I didn't need to know why anymore. It was OK that we were no longer together. I began to feel compassion for her and for the first time I "really saw her" and truly loved her. I realized all the times I didn't listen to her, I didn't see her, and even discounted her. And I am sorry for that. I began to wonder how many times in our relationship she found herself standing in front of the dresser wondering whether to write a note. I am grateful to have had her in my life, my perfect mirror, and I realize that in seeing her and loving her, I began to see myself, to love myself.

IT WAS MINE!   ALL OF IT!   AND IT DOES BELONG TO ME!!

I now find myself observing couples arguing and think, "Keep going; you will eventually be heard." As for my fellow frustrated grocery store patron and even the person giving me those beloved hand gestures, well if I'm lucky enough to meet them in the eyes I'd smile, and do my very best to convey—"you're loved." ○

Where everything connects

Jason Handler

Lost in a world where things don't seem to matter
I found a space in my heart where everything connects
Where ten thousand desires repressed in my chest
Dissolve in a breath and my mind can reflect on

How the space we forget
To acknowledge in breath
Humbly intersects

Over and over
We think and forget
the thoughts of the space
where every thing connects.

❂

Progression

Pat Cookinham

Winds of mellow warmth
wrap my soul in ecstasy.
Somewhere it's autumn.

Pristine flakes of snow
fill my being, cleanse my heart.
Time for me to go.

Holographic lines
bend backwards, ends connecting
pictures of nothing.

Awakening

Rachel Leach

I am lost in the past
in the craziness of the time
my mind races through the insanity
snap

my attention is diverted by a bright light
with an annoyed exhale
I return to my anxiety
my obsessive thoughts
to the world I know
snap

I'm distracted from my misery
For a moment I see the haze of the light
but my suffering entices me
calls me back to ruminate in its obscurity
snap

I hear my feet shuffling around the floor
I hear my solitude
my distraction
I feel alive, awake
but suffering creeps in
we begin to dance
it holds me and cradles me
just as it knows how and knows best
the music with it seems smooth and sweet
snap

I see the light over the dark pain's shoulder
I drop his hold of me
I begin to walk away
towards the light

He grabs my hand
trying to entice me to dance with him again
snap

my eyes don't divert this time
everything else falls away
fear
desire
Isolating shadows
the dance
nothing holds me or touches me
there is but one thing present,
the bright white light

Two Haiku

Wanda Rhodes

Illusion

My transparent life,
Silk threads, woven of nothing.
Cobwebs, squandered time.

Paradise Found

I drop the mirror.
My face shatters and dissolves,
the mask I don't need.

THE LADDER

The Ladder: The Ladder is a 108-foot sculpture (of a ladder) created by Hard Light Founder, Mark Griffin. At the annual Burning Man gathering in the Nevada Desert, it was erected to stand free and tall in the flat landscape. Rumor has it that some 400 people climbed the Ladder—and were never seen again!

The Ladder
Doug Ertman

Burning Man

Bob Schulenburg

From: Bob
To: Mark
Sent: 12/17/2005
Subject: Burning Man

Burning Man sounds like it was wonderful; I am delighted everything worked out so well, the fact you were able to stabilize the Ladder to the point people were able to climb it..."Wow, bravo!" And in a place where 35,000 people got to see it with no one being arrested or sued or flat out told "No, you cannot do that"...remarkable, congratulations!

The only way you were able to pull it off this year was by getting as close to pulling it off as you did last year, know what I mean? Meanwhile, in architectural, large-scale sculptural, memorial edifice, construction, completion, installation terms, a year is nothing! Good thing you were not relying on or cooperating with some external agency or institution. I am sure you would still be arguing about it with people who were opposed to the notion of such a thing even being considered, let alone approved, authorized and funded...

Thanks again for the taste of infinity today...

You know I love it,

Bob

From: Mark
To: Bob
Sent: 12/18/2005
Subject: Burning Man

Thanks Man,

Love, Mark

The Ladder

Lauren Freiman

Once upon a time there was a Great Guru and his twelve dharma warriors. In the month of August in the year two thousand and five A.D., they set out on a mission to raise a 108-foot free-standing ladder in the desert land of Black Rock City.[25] Legend has it that the ladder was climbed by some 400 people in the four days it stood. This is the story of the ladder.

The morning after they arrived, the warriors found their way to the designated ladder site, far out in deep space. They unloaded all of the pieces from the truck, and rung by rung began to construct the ladder. The sun was blazing and there was much discrepancy about how to raise the ladder, but eventually a plan was devised and soon followed by action. The six sections were lifted one at a time from the ground to a scaffolding where they were attached to and raised by a 120-foot crane. The ladder was built in this way from top to bottom. In the end, all 108 feet of the ladder were hanging by the crane, and then placed firmly into the base. By the following afternoon the ladder was detached from the crane, standing free.

Word spread around the city that a big ladder had been raised. People came from all corners searching for the ladder that was so far out in deep space. They came to climb, they came to watch, they came to see this fantastic beacon of light for themselves. Even the top officials of the city came. "What's it for?" the people asked. "What is it?" "Where does it go?" And the Guru and his dharma warriors happily replied.

When the sun went down and the city was aflame, the ladder looked most magnificent. From nearly all parts of the city an electrifying light could be seen rising straight up from the ground through the dark sky. It was perfectly symmetrical, elegant, and inconceivably powerful. It was a sight to behold.

Day in and day out the Guru and his dharma warriors sat by the glorious ladder. They sat in the scorching heat of the sun, the unruly windstorms, and the blackness of the night. They witnessed people of all walks of life climb up and down the ladder one after another, completely changed forever. For the climber, each step climbed meant layers and layers of

---

25 Black Rock City is a temporary city in the Nevada Desert that hosts the annual Burning Man celebration.

herself shed, until only what was most necessary remained. After a climb, she who reached the ground again was so much more herself than when she first ascended, that she was barely recognizable as the same person who began.

Many who climbed approached the ladder as if they were on a life or death mission and could not be stopped at any cost. For four days the climbing continued. It appeared that not a second passed without a person ascending or descending the ladder. Oftentimes there was a wait of twenty to thirty minutes to climb. People waited patiently for their turn.

There were all sorts of interesting stories about the people who came to see or climb the ladder. One woman said that she was an artist and had been drawing really tall ladders for the past year and a half but had no idea why. Once a photographer climbed to the top, crossed over to the other side of the ladder, and sat there peacefully taking pictures of the beautiful views of the city. Another time two naked people asked if they could climb the ladder together. The most famous was a woman who insisted on climbing the ladder at three in the morning and then proceeded to sit on the top rung for two hours. When later asked why she took so long to come down, the woman said that she was simply waiting for the sunrise.

The night after the man had burned, the time came for the ladder to be taken down. With joy and sorrow, the warriors set out for the last time into deep space. For four or five hours they waited for "Big Stick," one of the most popular men in the city, to arrive with the crane. After a gift of a few beers, "Big Stick" made his appearance and it was decided that the ladder would be lifted out of its base and lowered to the ground in one piece. Standing in awe below this great masterpiece changing its form, the warriors watched. Everything appeared to be going smoothly until the ladder reached about a 150-degree angle. Suddenly, the top section of the ladder broke off and flew to the ground with much force. One of the warriors almost became a ladder victim when the broken piece headed towards him, but fortunately he heard the third or fourth warning scream and quickly repositioned himself.

The ladder was determined easily repairable. Time stopped, and within what seemed like ten minutes, the ladder was taken apart into its original pieces and placed back into the big white truck. People were streaming from the city en masse as the desert wonderland came to a close. It was time for the Great Guru and his dharma warriors to make their exit. For the time being.

To be continued... ✺

Ladder 108

Paige Hetherington

Poem inspired by Summer Retreat, Taos, New Mexico 2005

My guru is my Papa
My mother is the Sea

I saw him at the airport
108 steps
"Are you afraid of heights?"

"Of course," I said.
Meditation. Desert, Snakes
Goddess' conversation

Endless sparkling ocean
Standing on the cliff of fear
All visions disappear.

No way to arrive but from such
    a high point?
Praise to the Eternal Spirit
For the grace waves that we surf

Water that cools
    The Fire that burns
        All pages
Guru heals all markings
Distillation - Alchemy.
Truth, Spirit Arise.

So'ham City

Fernando Escobar

I had no idea what I was getting into, but you know it's cool if Mark is going. Another art piece becoming another adventure. Black Rock City was an adventure that changed me forever. This is not much to say, since every time I see Mark I witness the rapid transformation in me in his presence, like it or not. I can't begin to explain, but just take my word for it. I was pretty much forced into a higher consciousness at that city. Making sure you don't get run over by an art car, discriminating between who's on drugs and who's not, and making sure you get down from the Ladder safely. Just kidding. All 400 of them not only got down in one piece but came down with a new light present within them. Black Rock City with Mark Griffin placed a new light within me. Believe me, I'm going back because this adventure was different.

I was very high, 108 feet high. We had just finished fifteen hours of putting up the Ladder. Mongoose unhooked the crane from the top section and the second ranger checked the strength of the wires holding it in place. We had assembled it by hooking the crane to the first two sections, and adding sections from the bottom, lifting it to the twenty-foot scaffold and having two others fasten it together. The magnificence of the 108 feet of shiny, airplane aluminum was breathtaking.

I looked straight up and wanted to climb but didn't know if I was allowed to. Why not? I went for it. The first twenty feet was to the scaffold, so I took a breath, contemplating my whole life for this one climb. I glanced at its dominance, its symbolism, its beauty, power, and more importantly, the simplicity of its one direction, straight up. "Climb! Climb!" something told me. Was it all right to climb it, with the artist I mean? Well, he'll tell me to stop if it isn't, so I took the first step. Everything came to mind at that moment, I'm sure a foreshadowing of how the moment at death would resonate. "So be it. I'll take you with me," I scolded my mind.

If I die, so be it. What better place and time to leave the body than with the Guru near me? From my understanding, the Ladder was not allowed to be climbed but my intentions were good and the drive within seemed to have forgotten that slight message from the Burning Man art director and staff. I'm half way there and my mind's volume overwhelmed me, "Get down! You will die! Live your life!" I took its advice, only the "live your life" part and continued. So'ham,[26] went each breath with each step as I admired the view of the city. I can see all the creativity that bombarded the flat, alkaline powdered grid called Black Rock City. Eight feet left and I'm done, but the mind trick about the last eight feet was that no wires were attached to it! So I dedicated the last eight feet to the Guru and abandoned myself. "SWAHA!!!"[27] as I held onto the last top bar of the Ladder with an empty mind. I felt close to enlightenment and an instant change in my life at that moment. Complete bliss. The Grace was bestowed by the Guru as I hear yelps and claps from my Hard Light friends down below.

I began reminiscing about the night before—the mind altering, neon lights around the city. I saw camps and people of all sorts. From sperm people (guys wearing hats shaped of sperm with sperm shaped motor vehicles), to meditation camps, nude same-sex and opposite-sex Hatha Yoga camps and workshops, art buses with built-in discos and bars, and in the center of it all was a 100-foot wooden man that is burned at the end of the week. Art cars, art bikes, art vehicles, costumes, and creativity. Words cannot describe the essence of Burning Man, and the mind cannot comprehend it, except to recognize its beauty. It was another planet out there full of creation, and the Ladder led the way to the infinite *Light*. I understood then why it can be so difficult to awaken through planes of consciousness without a light or a map to guide me, to show me what everything is or what direction to follow, especially getting back to the camp, to Hard Light, my friends and Mark. It took the morning sunrise on Wednesday to conclude we were at the 9:35 & Gestalt location[28] from the clock-shaped grid.

I began that Wednesday morning on my bicycle, exploring the terrain and seeing it all. I was destined not to miss a thing since it was all so beautiful to me. What the human race with peace, harmony, and full heart can do with land and complete freedom! I loved how the people of Black Rock City expressed themselves freely in an infinite number of ways. Not everyone, but about 99% of them were expressing the higher angels of compassion, honesty, and love. Some expressed fragility and vulnerability simply by going naked. I heard music; saw no govern-

---

26 So'ham is the vibration of God within each breath.
27 "Swaha" comes from "Om Swa Ha," the vibration of the three psychic nerves.
28 This was the street address of the Hard Light Camp in Black Rock City.

mental control, no money, just art. There was awareness of the earth and body, survival through the hot and dry day and chilling cold night, wind blowing white fogs of alkaline mist, and mountains surrounding us in the distance. It was a microcosmic city of the creative universe and the ocean of infinite consciousness: So'ham City.

I learned a lot from my adventure at Burning Man and raising the Ladder. It's not every lifetime I get to walk around with someone who talks to me and tells me the *Truth*. Everyone was happy and having so much fun which is such a rare sight in this day and age. But the greatest lesson of all came to me that week. A general rule when it came to artists and their art. Listen to the So'ham, stay away from the *artist's way*, and let Mark make his *masterpiece*. And one day, I will be different. ✪

Climbing the Ladder

Tim Maloney

What I find most remarkable about my relationship with Mark is that when my heart is pure and I ask for something with an earnest intention, free from grasping, it's as if he is a genie in a bottle and somehow, strangely manifests things very quickly for me, especially the money to go on two India trips with him. For someone with a terminal illness and living on a limited income, these trips were once-in a-lifetime events. The second trip was fascinating because of what happened after I asked Mark what someone who was grasping at going to India with him should do. When he said keep at it, I had no idea that within two days I would manifest the money to go from getting into a car wreck that was not my fault. I made it with an extra $40 in my pocket.

When I learned about Burning Man and decided that one day I would go and "be crazy too," I had little idea that Mark would make it happen in 2005...but he did. Again, like clockwork, the thought was put forth and the cash to go came as well. I had even offered a painting to Mark to take to burn for me, a Shiva with four heads with the caption, "I breathe for my guru." The day after I told Mark I wanted to go with him, I was purchasing my ticket. When I reached his art studio for the convoy, I was amused that I was one of three others who would be driving his artwork to Black Rock Mountain...I was amazed, bewildered, satiated, ecstatic.

Getting to be a "guard" for Mark's 108-foot ladder was the biggest thrill in my life because out of nowhere, I became this huge people person, interacting with everyone who was curious about his work. I was the fourth person to climb the ladder to the top. When I told Mark I wanted to do it, he asked if I was grounded. I casually said yes and then rode the bike off to the facilities knowing that I needed to ground myself more. I started running my mantra, Om Na Ma Shi Va Ya, over and over with each swift strike of the pedal, generating the rhythms of the fire. As I came back in view of my teacher I did not falter. I walked toward him and bowed and proceeded to climb the first twenty steps within twenty seconds...all the while reciting my mantra. See, I have a fear of heights and my guru knew this as I had gone sky diving for my 40th birthday to try and relinquish my one last great fear...and now I was on my way up to the top of this magnificent creation representing the enlightenment of any and all who tread the steep road toward that uncertainty, that abyss.

I marveled at my agility, I paused longer and with profound effect by wrapping my leg around the rungs and letting my hands dangle free sending reiki to the crescent shaped mass of blissful beings. As I reached toward the top I finally took one look down to acknowledge the cheers. This was when I had the urge to fly. It happened twice, but it was at that moment that I knew that I was forever transformed because my little hated timmy could not reign anymore, and I pushed away the thought of flying with my mantra. My mantra saved me from the ham that I am.

When I arrived on the ground I knelt at my teacher's feet and almost sobbed, but knew that would be grasping, so I took his gentle nudge and restlessly went to sit and ponder at what I had just done...my life was forever changed. There were no safety harnesses. This was life or death. Yet all these things are frivolous compared to what Mark has given me internally...this breath, this expansion in my heart, this life...all for the tasting. Mark is my everything. I breathe for Mark Griffin. ◉

Climbing the Ladder
Linda Horan

THE DARK VOYAGE

The Dark Voyage: Periodically, members of the Hard Light Sangha along with Guru Mark Griffin trek to India to experience her ancient secrets and mysteries. While the sun may be shining brightly all along the way, the shadow side is always close at hand.

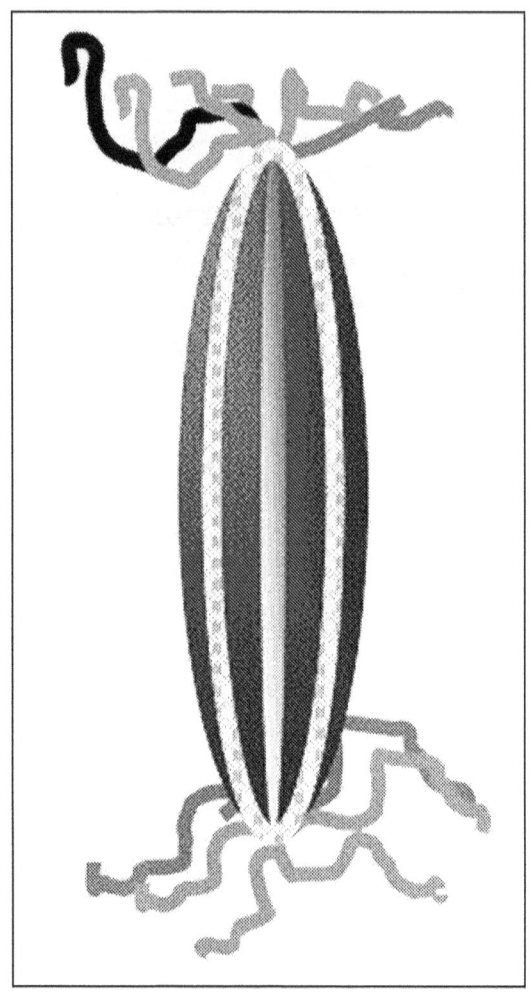

The Voyager
Pat Cookinham

Direct Report

Hal Barkhouse

> About a week after I got back to the farm in Weedpatch, Clementine, who lives a ways down the road, called up to find out what I did in India.

'Hi, Clem, like how fabulous was India?' (She's gotten to talking like they do in California.)

> "Hi Clemmie. Well, we sat around a while & practiced breathing."

'Clem, you better watch your breath around them people. What else did you do?'

> "We sat around a while & practiced thinking."

'Clem, that sure don't sound like you, who is this, really?'

> "Whup whup whup haw haw. You believe this? Some of the more advanced people there can actually breathe & think at the same time."

'Now Clem, my advice to you is: don't get carried away and do too much at once. Like, what else is fabulous in India?'

> "The car horns I like, sound like sheep or those birds from Africa. The streets are narrow & the traffic is fat. They all drive like, you seen those flocks of birds which zig & zag & circle around every which way, all in sync? They drive like that, like they all have the same thought, except once in a while one zigs when he should have zagged, then his car ends up looking like a bowling ball. The prices are low there. Say, listen Clemmie, I'll call you back; the chickens are starting to riot again. You behave yourself, or I'll have to spank you again."

'OOOOOOOH, is that fer sure? Bye now.' ○

How Will I Ever Survive INDIA?

Lauri Fraser

I'm a city girl. It wasn't my fault. I was born here. I love being in nature and looking at nature. I also hate bugs and outhouses, let alone having to go to the bathroom in a hole in the ground. I love culture and seeing how other people live. I also hate that there is poverty and that so many go to bed hungry. I leave in one week on a month-long journey with Mark Griffin, my meditation teacher of fifteen years, and a group of students from the sangha...

VARANASI, INDIA.

First entry, 5th day here:

> A baby has been crying somewhere outside of my room for the past 1/2hr. I've listened to it through my window from my bed, a sheet on a steel cot and a naked pillow which I've covered with my silk shawl. The voices I hear are the people working in and around the guesthouse where I'm staying. Cooks clanging pots and pans, boys and men talking, a television playing either Indian news, or the latest Cricket match. Indians love Cricket and Pakistan was playing India so the heat was on. I can hear someone knocking at the guesthouse door. No one answers. Continuous knocking. Someone sweeps. The baby is quiet. I am resting before the 4th day of meditation resumes. The stairs to the Raja Ghat (the meditation hall) also lead down to the Ganges River where one can bathe to rid themselves of past sins and Karma. You must, however, share the water with the cows, waste, and ash from the crematorium, not to mention the occasional corpse.
>
> It is said that Lord Shiva dove from the 7th plane of existence into the ocean and his head came up (along with the rest of him) from the Ganges, and this place called Varanasi (Benares), India has been sacred ever since. This, the oldest continuously inhabited city in the world, is home to the holiest, the seekers, the rich, the poor and the plain, but one thing is certain. The veil is sheer and the psychic energy runs hot and high here. All I have to do is think of something and there it is. From wishing there were eggs on my plate instead of oatmeal (the little Indian boy smiled and bowed his head as he changed my plate, without

me saying a word) at breakfast, to a question answered an instant after it appears in my thoughts.

The chanting is constant as are the celebrations honoring Lord Shiva, for this is the week before Shivaratri, the day Shiva kissed this part of the earth. All the great masters have passed through Varanasi. It is a vortex. Buddha first spoke the truth in Sarnath. Christ, Moses, the great lineage of the Siddhas and probably every important Lineage of all the different faiths touched down here on their journey.

Okay, so here I am. What am I doing here? I may not know the answer for quite some time, but for now it is where I'm supposed to be. Just part of the journey. The search for truth and self. Abandon the ego here they say. Okay. Sure. But it keeps finding its way back. Such is life. This one, anyway. ✺

Fear and Loathing in India

Brian Stephens

Exit the plane and bam! It hits me like a ton of bricks, I'm back in India. God help me. I think I've made a terrible mistake.

That smell of smoke, where the *!#*%* is that smell coming from because it seems to be everywhere? Of course, that's just my imagination again. Surely the smoke is just local to the airport area, and when we make it to the backwoods of India the smell will subside. It has to, because if it doesn't I'm gonna freak out.

I'm back in India for the second time in two years. What? How could this be? Thought for sure I would never step foot in India again, yet here I am. This is not happening. This is not happening.

Feels like I never left India from the first trip. Maybe I never did leave, maybe the last two years back in the US has been some kind of hyper-reality dream. Four years ago when I joined Hard Light that kind of hyper-reality dream talk would have sounded like good old fashioned crazy talk and now it doesn't—and that's the scariest part of all.

The first India trip was brutal. Probably got sick from the food, my body's not used to the bacteria in India. I still had chronic fatigue back in those days. Throw on top of that some funky Indian bacteria in the digestive system and it was a hypochondriac's nightmare come to life. I was white as a ghost for four days. Took two full doses of penicillin and still barely made it back to the states with my guts intact. It's best not to think about it, especially since I'm here again and I have to eat sometime.

If being sick was not enough, my first India trip included seven days in Varanasi. Mark says, "Varanasi is Shiva, the people who live there aren't really people anymore, they're something else..." What else, I don't know and don't want to know, but he's gonna tell me anyway. "The citizens of Varanasi are portals, beings from the upper and lower planes move through them like elevators." What the *!#*%*? Thanks Mark, thanks for blowing my mind, once again. Here I am just some hillbilly from Missouri sitting in a room with an enlightened guy who seems to enjoy telling ghost stories and freaking me out. Mark doesn't do it on purpose; he just overestimates my fragile grip on reality these days.

We're kicking off this little "vacation" with a three-day meditation intensive in Ganeshpuri. We're in the bus heading off to the Land of Oz, the whole Hard Light gang. Everyone seems to be having fun except yours truly. I'm fighting the urge to jump from the moving bus and make a run for it. When am I going to get sick? It's my new mantra. Thank God I brought my music. Without tunes I could not be held responsible for my actions.

By the way, how did I end up in Hard Light? I never looked for a meditation teacher. I'm not a particularly good person. What gives? Don't you have to at least try to help people before you get this kind of a break? Till meeting Mark, two thoughts dominated my waking hours—how can I make more money and how can I date more hot chicks? When I'm at my best it feels like I caught the biggest break anybody can catch. But I'm not at my best right now. I don't feel lucky. I feel like I've been drafted into the army and sent overseas on assignment. But I don't get to know the assignment because that kind of information is on a need-to-know basis, and the class dunce doesn't need to know.

When overcome by a rare moment of honest self reflection, what bothers me most is that Mark actually let me join Hard Light. Not only that, he lets me keep coming to the meetings. Are they really that desperate for members? Woody Allen (quoting Grouch Marx) said it best, "I would never want to belong to any club that would have someone like me for a member."

Back to the problem at hand, I'm in India, I have a history of getting really sick in India, and I'm going be here for two weeks—an eternity. The waiting is torture. Let's get it over with. If I would just get sick I wouldn't have to worry anymore about getting sick. Like anything, thinking about the prospect is far worse than the actual event. It has to be. My God, have I always been this neurotic?

Day three in Ganeshpuri and finally, finally, finally, it happens. What's that? A twinge of pain in my stomach, the feeling of nausea, beads of sweat rolling down my forehead, lightheadedness, weakness—it's back. The wait is finally over. The Indian bacteria are once again waging a full-out assault on my immune system. I made the mistake of eating lettuce for lunch yesterday. You aren't allowed to make mistakes in India. Only one way to cope, turn up the Rolling Stones, "... here it comes, here it comes, here it comes, here it comes, here comes your nineteenth nervous breakdown."

Thankfully, the horrible wait is over. I'm sick again but at least now I can relax and enjoy myself. ✪

India 2003

Marcelle Marshall

India has captured my heart.
If I sit down and listen very carefully, I begin to notice a beautiful play.
If I let my heart linger with the atmosphere around me, I notice a
synchronistic melody between everything.
It's the sweetness of Saints that
live here. An atomic bomb of God's love.

I sit quietly with this hush cloud of pure reality,
delighted by its sweetness it makes me cry
caught by Grace
Beyond time and space
Once there, always there...

into the ganga

Lauren Freiman

all i know is that i need to go in the water.

i want to immerse myself in the water until it saturates every molecule of my being.

> in the still emptiness
> i race across the sand
> and anxiously look for a pathway in

> but then there's trash, and there's dirt, and maybe even disease

> my path in is being blocked

> after a second of doubt and fear
> i gently cross over to the other side

freedom

> the path is clear
> all i have to do now is
> walk in
> but somehow i'm not quite sure how.

> a solid black rock rears its head thru the passing tides
> oh this must be the way!
> i jump for the rock because i long ago decided that there was no other option than

to go in

> i land but i'm not in deep enough yet

> another rock appears
> further in towards the center of the racing, ravenous water

> i leap, and land with my entire body

> what about now?

i ask,
am i in deep enough now?

      the rocks have disappeared

i surrender

      laying on my back facing the sky
      listening to mySelf, the ganga

suddenly
there is no difference
the sky
the water
mySelf
without separation.

i exhale

      there is nowhere to go
      i am everywhere i need to be
      finally, the search is over.

finally,
peace.

Pictures of India

Mandy Hooper

Meditation...how many still do not know what kind of tool that is. If this were all that India ever shared with us, it would be too much. And who thanks India? The Saints and will-be Saints. The Cows thank India.

There was a time when I thought India was far away. The depth and breadth of India may be translated into how deeply your consciousness can reach into the artful symbolism of pure raw data layered within. As we may do a dance to Lord Shiva expressing the movement of the kundalini, so may each symbol...layered in stone, music, food, incense, fabrics...meanings behind each sight, sound, taste, touch, and smell.

Her clothing is so luscious, that when I drape garments from India around me, I feel soft and subtle again. I feel lovely.

The secret mouth of India...ignores you until you open your heart to her. Then she awaits your grace-filled entrance.

Why does the tree look like that, giant arms outstretched, unusually giving and heartfelt? I see them sit in meditation at her base. Her limbs reaching out. It feels like the tree is the Goddess Durga, Goddess of Life and Death, Love and Justice. She does not look Fierce now...but embracing everyone with many loving arms. I can't wait to be hugged... when I see that tree.

I see the River Ganges...it is empty and blue and fresh and I want to dive in it. Later I see it is a dark green, and its path winds around like a snake.

Who carved those magnificent things out of the Rock? Stories translate into pictures there. It will not be lost in me. Stone Stories.

I see the Statue of Lord Shiva standing tall. How tall is he? I wonder how it would be to stand at one with him.

Mark...Our Teacher is in India, with the sangha.

Awaiting His arrival, great preparation and excitement. They love him but most do not know who he is yet, arising on the Inside. But we all want to align ourselves with a Man...Being. Because of men and women being...we too shall arise one day.

Nityananda says...the best Cobras have the subtle pranic breath.

They have linked your picture with flowers to Nityananda's.

I see He sits on the platform with others and they are all in Samadhi...

> *Wait a minute...*
> *How often do things like this happen,*
> *I have never read about this happening.*
> *What kinds of vibrations are created then?*
> *Devotees meditate below the four symbolic steps*
> *that lead up to them*
> *Something Wonderful happened that day*

I understand when I see these things. People do attain Samadhi and come together. They sit in the Absolute Timelessness of Wherever their Pure State of Consciousness takes them. As we meditate with Mark in his state of Nirvikalpa Samadhi, we get high as he excites our subtle senses and gives us a sense of contact.

It takes someone in the Heart Beat of Shaktipat to appreciate certain subtle things. Like a trip to India with your teacher. His hands are ripe and full of wisdom, but I cannot read them. It takes a Master to infuse that seed. And that seed is placed within your system by the true Alchemist.

> *The river speaks, water never sleeps and neither do you*
> *The river is the force within*
> *A symbol of the middle path*
> *Deeper and ever deeper and ever deeper*
> *Everyone must turn one day and slide in*
> *And on that day you will Arise like a waterfall in the center of your own river*

With no teacher, many times we tremble in fear or we just miss a turn and stop arising with the same act of will we used to engage it. Therefore Grace be our teacher, and his name is Mark.

To the Rush of

~ **Victory** ~

I wanted to tell you something, and I ran and ran to say…I was in India today. ✺

Second Time Around

Jan Myers

It is very difficult for me to write about India this time around. After the first visit, the words just flowed. I couldn't wait to share with everyone! Something was different this time. It was so personal. I haven't even finished processing it myself. Truthfully, I don't know if I ever will.

I did have two "only in India" experiences. The first one happened one evening as we were leaving the temple. I heard a young Indian woman call out "Janet." Although I am known as "Jan" by Hard Light members and most of my friends, Janet is my birth name. I had never met this woman before. When I acknowledged her, she introduced me to her family and her baby son. She asked how I liked Ganeshpuri and told me about herself, what she was studying, and invited me to visit her school sometime. She touched my heart in ways that I can't describe. She was so genuinely interested in me and sharing herself with me. Her warmth and friendliness were amazing!

The second experience happened on the day that the women in our group were all wearing their red saris. A tiny woman shopkeeper named Vijaya came up to me, touched my arm, and asked me to come with her and she would help me "fix" my sari. We immediately walked to her store and went into the back, where she carefully redressed me and taught me how to do the sari myself. Granted, I probably had the "sorriest sari" in the group, but I still felt blessed that she cared enough to help me out. After this, Van and I would see her almost daily during our walks back and forth from our Guest House. On the night that our bus returned from the Yatra, she was waiting there to meet us. She covered my eyes from behind to surprise me, then gave us a big "welcome back" hug!

These two women were examples of the love and warmth that Ganeshpuri showed me. There is an energy there that I have experienced nowhere else. I miss it. ✪

Oh, What's so Great about India?

Hal Barkhouse

How did I benefit most from the India tour?

My biggest benefit came from meeting some of the Masters. It's July 20, four months after the tour, and what sticks with me the most is getting to meditate with them.

With Zar Zar Zarbak in his mosque for half an hour. A master of the seven chakras and kundalini, the inside of his mosque looks just like the seven chakras, especially the dome. A Bonneville Salt Flats for the three rivers.

With Meher Baba in the Cosmic Cave at Ellora and again with him in Meherabad. A master of love, His silence overwhelms the loudest sounds you can ever hear.

An all night meditation at Ganeshpuri with Nityananda, Muktananda, and many more, too many to name; they all came there to be with Mark. ✪

India Yatra 2005

Vanig Torikian

Two sheets of yellow paper with the word AWAKEN at the top; "To make sure you don't forget to write a story about our last trip to India," says Mark, as he hands them to the few delinquents.

Being a card-carrying member of that group, I quickly take out a pen, energized by this newly-found inspiration and start writing: "...you bring the Brie, I'll bring the whine." My past failed attempts at bribing a teacher or two in high school, to be excused from homework, flash before my eyes, as I catch myself talking to Mark in my head saying: "Mark, do I really *HAVE* to do this?" when out of nowhere, I would say about four degrees left of my Sushumna, I hear Mark's voice: "Do it or I will crush you like a coconut, you nut."

"...ummm, may I have two more sheets please? Thank you."

I thought the word AWAKEN on the yellow sheet Mark gave us was meant to be a directive for enlightenment, not a strategy to keep me awake every night until I wrote my story. It's not that I had forgotten to write it you see; it's just that I've been skillfully delaying engaging my mind on the topic, because I find it very hard to write about the trip this time around. Nothing outwardly out of the ordinary happened to me on this trip, no specific incident or event that I would consider worthy of sharing. I keep digging and searching and probing my memory in desperation to find something, anything, but keep coming up with twelve lbs of coded messages I can't decipher yet and seven ounces of guilt. Guilt has a short shelf life they say and quickly turns to blame. If that is the case, then I choose to blame Jan, who failed miserably at offering the necessary drama, crisis and misfortune she had spoiled me with during our trip to Varanasi two years ago. No burns, no falls, no broken bones; the nerve some people have. She should be ashamed of herself.

What to write about then? Will some observations about the trip appease the Gods of Literature perhaps? I sure hope so.

What was different about this trip compared to the last? Was it less exciting? Had the novelty of the culture and environment worn off? Was the second trip less of a cultural shock perhaps? Not really. It wasn't that much of a cultural shock to me in the first place. Even though Indian culture and lifestyle are unique, a lot of what I experienced there reminded me of Lebanon, where I was born and lived for nineteen years. The Kurdish people in Lebanon with their traditional attire, similar though not as colorful as the Indians', the poverty, the filth, the contrast between the poor and the wealthy (on a much smaller scale of course), the clash between east and west, the traffic, the incessant honking, the sounds and smells, were all part of my daily life growing up. What I find different about India is that special connection to God I feel while there. It seems like the distance of three feet to enlightenment anywhere else in the world is shorter in India for some mysterious reason. There's an undeniable intensity to one's spiritual pulse there and one feels a natural urge to face oneself, as the distractions of the western lifestyle aren't as intrusive.

So what was different about this trip? If the Varanasi trip was about God in heaven, I would say the Ganeshpuri trip for me was about God on earth. Maybe that doesn't make much sense to you, but I don't know how else to explain. There was something about Ganeshpuri that felt like home. Everywhere I turned, there was God. Time felt more vertical than horizontal. Looking back, I realize everything and everybody there served as a teacher: the people, the buildings, the cows, the dogs, the birds, the trees, the music, the heat, the cold, the food. I felt deep, silent communication behind a nod, a wink, a smile, a touch, a hello, a gaze, a sigh, a taste, a hug. I witnessed compassion, kindness and love and felt inspired and free. I witnessed selfishness and rude behavior, and knew how not to be. I saw the dedication and contentment of the locals and was humbled. If the Varanasi retreat was more about individual quest, the Ganeshpuri retreat seemed to have more of a group quality, as if we were on a group mission, and I became aware of our interconnectedness. Spiritual goals were important and yet not important. All that mattered was that we were there, basking in that energy, soaking it all in, just being.

And if you asked me would I move to Ganeshpuri to live, I would grin, clear my throat and sing: "I left my heart…in Ganeshpuri…"

Eat your heart out Mr. Bennett. ✺

Out of India

Lauri Fraser

I am told that people get a calling to go to certain places. India is one of those places. Me, I had no calling to go to India but it was the right time for this sort of a trip. Work was steady. I was not in a relationship. Had I been, and had my love looked over at me and said, "I love you and I'm taking you to India," I would have said, "Go fish." I love you Tahiti? Yes. I love you Italy? Yes. But India? No! This, however, was the time to go. Mark Griffin, my meditation teacher of fifteen years, was taking a group of his students on a month-long trip that consisted of visiting sacred sights, meditating for days on end, and culminating with a fire ceremony (Yagna) put on by Brahman priests—a most difficult thing for a Western guy to attain unless of course that Western guy happens to be Mark Griffin. I had a lot of fear about going to a place where children are suffering and poverty is everywhere. What if I got lost? What about the bugs? What if I got sick? What if I got malaria! I was fearful of so many things, one of which was no western toilets. Going to the bathroom in a hole in the ground was not this city girl's idea of relief. Looking into the eyes of hunger and poverty was not big on my list either.

Although I would meet everyone there, I was alone for now. Politically it was not the time to travel. It was late February 2003. Word had it that the people of the world, or parts of it anyway, were changing their opinion of Americans. We were warned not to have any sort of flags or emblems on our luggage. I decided it couldn't hurt to take those instructions seriously.

When I got to the airport there were Indian Military everywhere...and cows everywhere else. We were greeted with smiles and helped onto buses for the next leg of our journey. No animosity towards Americans.

Varanasi is the oldest continually-inhabited city in the world. Three million people in a city the size of Santa Monica. Could you exhale so that I can inhale?

Understand, the country is poor. It takes $3,500.00 to feed, house, and clothe a family for a year. No trash dumps. Hardly any trash cans. No traffic lights. No stop signs. Watching the traffic move is like an orchestrated dance, conducted by a pecking order of horns and bells. Bikes, rickshaws, tuk-tuks, motorcycles, cars, trucks, buses, people and cows. Hardly any accidents. In fact, in India, if you're not careful, crossing the road can propel you right into your next life. Oh, and monkeys. (They have been known to slap you on the head and steal your backpack. Yes! They can smell a tourist three miles away.)

The Indians Love to negotiate. It's part of their culture. I just wanted to pay the price. I was sick of haggling, but they wouldn't let me. You say, "How much?" and you get your wallet out ready to pay whatever they ask. They know this. They know you're weary. They say, "One thousand dollars." "For an incense burner?! I wouldn't pay over 20." "Oh goody. Nineteen ninety-nine. Very special. You'll never see another one like it." "Really?" "Oh. It's absolutely positively perfectly." They love to use three adverbs in a row. Absolutely positively perfectly is a common one.

There were beggars everywhere, but they would smile at you instead of just beg. And if you said, "No, Namaste" (which means no, but peace my friend...sort of), they would usually put their hands in prayer and go away...for a while anyway.

India was a magnificent sight to see. The architecture was amazing and so old. To be so present in a place of such history was really something. India is in your face. Everything happens at the same time. It's as though there aren't any walls separating life. A person is suffering at the same time a person is praying, at the same time a person is marrying at the same time a person is getting cremated. It's all right there.

I cried every day, over the poverty and the suffering children. Also, every day, as I walked down the steps to meditate I would pass the same woman. She had leprosy and almost no nose. She would tilt her head to one side with a sad look on her face as she held an old tin cup out to me. I would put something in the cup and then go back to my room and cry. One of the older women on the trip asked me how I was doing, and I said awful and told her about the old woman. "What could I do for her? I feel like such a greedy American. I have so much and..." She interrupted me and said, "You can look in her eyes, and with everything you've got you can give her your smile, with every bit of good energy that you can muster up." Oh, sure. Easy for you to say with your Bloomingdale's underwear and your iPod.

The next morning as I descended the steep stairs, I could see her sitting there. I realized that up to this point, I hadn't looked at her. I had put money in the cup each day but never looked into her eyes. I was afraid. I took a breath and thought of nothing but the purest intention of beauty and goodness meant just for her and I smiled my best possible smile. My heart was beating so fast. I kept smiling. Then she broke open this most beautiful smile right back at me and her eyes sparkled and I went right back up to my room and I cried. But it was a different sort of cry this time.

It was a very special time in India. It was Shivaratri. Thousands of people come from all over the world to be at the foot of the Ganges River for Shivaratri.

Temples were everywhere and we were most fortunate to be taken on a tour by Shivananda, a Polish scholar fluent in Sanskrit. These were not your normal temples. No, we were taken on a Raiders-of-the-Lost-Ark sort of tour. He was not a tour guide, but he knew where all the sacred temples were. Under walkways, and through rock tunnels. We eventually made our way down to a temple on the River Ganges. This was where I had to make haste and get back to the hotel in the middle of town to catch a plane to Bangkok. I was to travel with a friend, who had been my roommate for this trip. We had decided to go to Thailand on the way back to America. I looked around but she was not with the group and it was time to go so we could make the long trek to the airport. I sent one of the kids back to look for her, but he returned without her and I started to get a little nervous.

This was Shivaratri and the city was even crazier than usual and I was by myself all of a sudden.

I left to go back to the hotel. I walked along the Ganges because that was my only source of reference. I played like I was chanting and praying and was hardly bothered by anyone. Suddenly I was lost. I had to get back to the hotel. I hopped on a rickshaw. As we made our way down narrow, rocky streets towards the hotel, the pollution and the soot were very thick. I had on a white shirt with flowers in my hair, a blessing from the priest of the last temple we visited. Every time I went into a temple I was blessed, blessed so many times I'm sure I was ordained by association.

As the rickshaw picked up speed I noticed another rickshaw approaching. Riding in the seat was a beautiful Indian woman in a brilliantly orange-colored sari along with her son who had perfect white teeth. Indian mouths seem to be filled with either old rotted pointed teeth or perfect white teeth. The woman had a sheer orange shawl that matched and it was draped lightly over her nose and mouth. Walking on the side of the road was a Muslim woman in her burqa, also with her son, both in black, and she was completely covered by her matching black shawl. It covered everything but her eyes. Then there was me. I had on my wreath of flowers and my shawl that I had only just removed from my shoulders to wrap over my nose and mouth because it was so dusty. My choice to cover my face or not.

As I sat in the rickshaw, both the women and I had a dance going on with our eyes. Each just looking, observing. For a moment, everything went into slow motion and there was just the three of us. She's looking at me; I'm looking at her, the two of them looking at each other then back to me. Not Indian, Muslim, American. Just three women, all living different lives, but women just the same.

I had to catch my breath. I felt almost claustrophobic. What was so different about me? I was a free woman. I had my freedom. Sweet freedom.

We boarded the plane. I was on Air India, while SARS[29] was on China Air. I left the U.S. grateful for all that I have in my life. I returned grateful for tap water and an infrastructure. ✪

---

29 SARS (Severe Acute Respiratory Syndrome) is a virus that killed 774 people in 2002/2003.

Varanasi

Christinea Johnson

...from another time, another place.

Chaos everywhere.
Holiness everywhere.
The River...
Shiva's river taking souls home...
Back to the One source.
Thru every breath.
Thru every fire.
Ghat, ghat, ghat.
Steps to birth.
Steps to death.
Steps to home.
Ghat, ghat, ghat.

The Raja Ghat

Charles Lonsdale

I stand on the balcony above the Raja Ghat looking out at the sweeping curve of the Ganga River. On the eastern shore, stone and cement buildings crowd the water's edge. To the west, two miles of flood plane, mostly sand and silt, some seasonal vegetation. The river, about a half mile wide, swings lazily along the shore, moving north. Dozens of small boats ferry people from ghat to ghat and across the river.

In the distant haze, a massive three story Maha-mandap has been erected for the coming Shivaratri celebration. A very loud loudspeaker calls out prayers and songs from the mandap. Mystical sounds waft across the river.

The sun sets gently upon the landscape. Soft amber light filters through the evening haze. Blackbirds circle above, searching for a nightly roost. A conch blows at a nearby temple calling devotees to evening prayer. Below me, along the waterfront, children play catch with a ball; a calf wails for its caretaker. Small fires are lit, food is prepared, a priest lights incense and a huge candelabra for arati.[30] Shadows deepen, voices soften. Soon the Sun sinks crimson at the western edge. Tranquility saturates the deepening night.

The ground beneath me seems to sway. It is as if I am on the deck of a small boat rocking gently on shore swells. I am a little dizzy, intoxicated by new sounds and smells, ancient mystery. It feels as though the world before me will fall away, and reveal...I know not what. I soak in peace, sweet irresistible peace. ✪

---

[30] Arati, a ritual performed before meditations, ceremonies and on many other occasions, is used to bring blessings and ward off evil. It is also called "waving of lights."

Varanasi Blues

Doug Ertman

We were ten minutes outside of Varanasi when the bad omen happened. It was a twelve-hour train ride from Delhi on the Shivganga Express, and as first light dawned I opened the drapes to take in the passing view. What I saw was people shitting. And not just a few people, either. Whole neighborhoods, it seemed, turned out for group evacuation of their bowels at daybreak. Evidently the land nearest the railroad tracks was understood as the place to go, and the people seemed oblivious to the total lack of privacy as the train rocked past. This was foreshadowing, the earliest expression of a shit-related theme—one that would reemerge frequently throughout the trip.

As the light grew the number of people shitting decreased, giving way to empty, pastoral fields and crops. I had my face pressed against the window taking in the landscape when I saw a kid standing by the side of the tracks watching the train go by. He looked about thirteen, and as he drew back his right hand in an unmistakable pitcher's windup, his eyes rolled back crazily.

SMASH! His rock hit the outer train window two inches from my head, and I jerked backward in shock, staring at the thin cracks radiating from the impact point. I summoned the porter and showed him the destruction. He shrugged his shoulders and smiled sheepishly—giving me a "happens all the time, nothing we can do about it" look.

I was shaken at how close I had come to serious damage. Could the kid see me through the window? Should I take it personally? Was he making a statement, waiting for the only first class car to throw his rock? Was it because I was Caucasian, "wealthy," an unwanted foreigner, or was it a violent, random act of adolescent vandalism? Which answer was more troubling? "Welcome to Varanasi," I told myself.

It was my second visit. Two years earlier I flew in with the Hard Light meditation group and was bussed straight to the Clark, a Raj-era five star hotel. But a night at the Clark costs enough to feed an Indian family for a year, and I was determined to live more humbly on this trip. For instance, my wife Setsuko and I had chosen to take the train instead of flying from Delhi. True, we were in first class, but this was our first train journey in India. Eventually we discovered that second class was fine, and even third class, with narrow bunks stacked three to the wall submarine-style, was tolerable.

We decided the humble human-powered bicycle rickshaw was the way to get to our hotel, and by some miracle we negotiated a fair price. The leisurely pace of the rickshaw gives you a chance to take in your environment, to ease into your surroundings. It gives you time to think things like, "I've made a terrible mistake. I'm going to die here and no one will ever know. Where are we? Why did I come here? How do I know the driver is taking me where I said I wanted to go? How do we know we won't end up as captives somewhere, forced to assemble handicrafts, our ATM accounts drained at gunpoint?"

Riding through Varanasi on a bicycle rickshaw is like following Virgil into the lower circles of hell. The filth, poverty, and chaos are overwhelming. You'll see free range cattle in the city, big cows and enormous bulls with horns, in the road, in your face. Beggars. Pollution. Decay. Curious locals staring at you. Motorized rickshaws, scooters, motorcycles, cars, trucks, busses, driven homicidally and suicidally, at top speed, horns blaring, belching fumes.

As you get closer to the old city and the river, there are traffic roundabouts that look like slow motion tornados, watched over by braces of lounging police wielding long wooden sticks. This is where we ran down our first pedestrian. A portly, middle-aged matron in a sari actually bounced off the wheels of our rickshaw and bitterly cursed our driver.

The Ganges is the end of the line, the lanes becoming so narrow, congested and steep that even a bicycle rickshaw becomes impractical. Time to don our backpacks and hoof it the rest of the way to our hotel. Walking along the ghats, endless rows of steep steps leading down to the holy, polluted river, we are fresh meat for the touts. Everyone is selling something. The beggars sell guilt, and the rest sell lodging, food, hashish, jewelry, annoying reed instruments demonstrated in your ear, and, especially, boat rides.

Every fifty feet there is a boat entrepreneur who is convinced that you have come half way around the world for the express purpose of buying a ride on his boat, perhaps to better observe the corpses of dead animals and people that float by occasionally on the sacred filthy river. You must want a boat, he thinks. You need a boat. You're dying to have a boat. And not just any boat: his boat. He has only to ask. And so he does, favoring a direct approach that shows a remarkable linguistic economy.

"You want boat?" he asks. And then delivers the deal closer: "Is best time." The twentieth time you exit your hotel to go to the meditation hall you would think that, by now, the locals would know your preferences: ix-nay on the oat-bay. Not aquatically inclined. Confirmed pedestrian. But hope springs eternal every fifty feet in the form of a question: "You want boat?"

Our hotel was right on the Ganges, our room a fifth floor walkup on the rooftop, with an expansive view. From the fourth floor restaurant deck we could see the Ganges from north to south, including the smoke rising from the funeral pyres upriver. The flood plain stretching out behind the river was enormous. In the high season the water rises thirty feet, obliterating the giant sandbar where a huge number of holy men were having a camping jamboree. They were mighty organized over there. In the middle of a dry riverbed they had enough electricity to power loudspeakers and neon lights flashing in carnival patterns. Think Hindu meets Las Vegas: "Loosest slots on the Ganges."

Every budget hotel room in India is required to have at least one totally irrational architectural feature, and we quickly found ours in the bathroom: whimsical toilet placement, with insufficient legroom. Let's just say that adopting a less conventional, perpendicular position was the only way to sit down to business. Much of India seems to be a code-free zone when it comes to construction, and our five flights of stairs to the rooftop were treacherously steep and uneven.

It was only later in the evening that we discovered a serious drawback to our penthouse. Four floors of plumbing below us vented at the rooftop, right outside our room, making certain hours of the day a pungent affair.

This unwelcome revelation was somewhat mitigated by a view of the wild monkeys on adjacent buildings, who typically travel from rooftop to rooftop as they patrol their territory. They casually perform astounding acrobatics, scaling four and five-story buildings using only window ledges and drainpipes, some with babies clinging to their stomachs.

The monkeys are clever enough to distinguish between the local Indian population and the tourists, and do they ever take liberties with the latter. We found out the hard way that they considered our rooftop their territory. Setsuko was sitting quietly in a rooftop chair looking at the river, when a mated pair of monkeys snuck up behind her. The male smacked her on the back of the head, while the female screamed and gestured threateningly, and then they stole her water bottle.

Paying hotel guests weren't the only primates with rooftop accommodations. I opened my door at 4 a.m. to find two whole simian families huddled together, babies sandwiched between adults for warmth, seven monkeys in all. I considered writing some advertising copy for our hotel. "Rooftop rooms with view of the Ganges. Hot and cold running attack monkeys. Complimentary smell of sewage…"

I spent quite a bit of time at our fourth floor restaurant, seeing if it was possible to eat $2 worth of food without stuffing myself to the point of injury. The Indian food was terrific. I quickly developed an addiction to coffee lassis, a plain yogurt drink with a shot of espresso thrown in. Here's a hot tip: even if you're tired of it, stick to the Indian food in Varanasi. Under no circumstances should you order spaghetti.

In our frequent five-minute walks along the river between the hotel and the meditation hall, we inevitably found our senses assaulted with the stench of human urine and the sight of human excrement. It's easy to become frustrated at the dysfunction of a society that has failed, in 10,000 years, to come to agreement about not using the sidewalk as a toilet. There is an alternative route: the lanes in back of the river.

The lanes are truly medieval. Dark, winding and beckoning, they are full of animals and pedestrians, interesting shops and shopkeepers, and little miniature sacred spots that are no more than blessed holes in the wall, with statues of deities so old and worn that it is impossible to tell anymore who or what they represent.

Another medieval aspect of the lanes—and here our foreshadowed theme reappears in all its glory—is the virtual feces festival found there. Not human, thankfully. Cow, bull, goat, dog, donkey, goose and chicken shit abound. In the Monty Python movie *The Holy Grail*, it is said you can recognize the king "because he hasn't got shit all over him!" In Varanasi, it's impossible to tell who is king. I speak from personal experience of being caught in the lanes unavoidably close to the business end of a water buffalo. Those pants are never going to be the same.

Something else to watch for in the lanes: madmen on motorcycles trying to run down the young, the innocent, the old and the lame. Everything flees before them except the cows, because they're...well, sacred cows. In fact, the centuries mix in the picture of giant horned cattle, agrarian and timeless, sitting nonchalantly in front of businesses advertising Internet connections and long distance telephone service. It is said that Varanasi is the oldest continuously inhabited city in India, eight or ten or even twelve thousand years old. Certainly some of the shops could be that old, and possibly some of the shopkeepers.

The night before our meditation event was not restful. Setsuko had a constant, hacking, viral cough so severe that even codeine wasn't helping. At 2 a.m., just as I was finally falling asleep, the thousand-strong United Brotherhood of Scroungy River Dogs convened to redraw their territorial boundaries through an orderly process of howling and snarling. It really wasn't much of a shock when, at 3:40 a.m., the fanatics at Hindu Vegas cranked up their considerable sound system and began blasting mantras[31] into the darkness. My heart filled with bitterness, and I knew that this meditation retreat would be like so many others: first the sleep deprivation, and then the illness that was sure to follow.

And just why were we here of all places, jetlagged, culture shocked, sick, so far from home, at such great expense, in such great filth? It was not for lack of trying to lure our teacher to someplace, anyplace else. "What about Paris?" I often broadly hint, or "I hear Florence is lovely this time of year." But no. Mark unerringly heads for Varanasi, Kashi, Benares—a place so full of squalor it requires three names.

In the spiritual game, to receive blessings, you go where the teachers are

---

31 Mantras are sacred words or sounds invested with the power to transform and protect the one who repeats them.

who can generate them. If they call a meeting on the far side of the moon, you try your best to get there. Apparently the far side of the moon was booked, and we had to settle for the far side of the earth. We were here because the teacher was here.

It is said that the Guru names a time and a place, and the student shows up. It's not that simple. For one thing, the student whines quite a bit first.

I'm not going to say much about my experience in the yagna, the fire ceremony. I would rather explore the consequences, the impact of attending such an event. It is true that I sat in meditation for five days in a stone temple, watching half-naked Brahmin priests chant the 10,000 names of Shiva ten times over while consigning innocent produce to a fiery death. After watching them burn every fruit, nut and legume in the place, I half expected them to move on to the furniture and then jump in themselves.

There should probably be a word other than meditation to describe showing up and enduring the onslaught of transformational energy that emerges through a real teacher, a so-called shaktipat guru. There is always the lurking specter of the secular meaning of meditation, synonymous with the "relaxation response." As in, "Go to your happy place, think of fluffy white clouds and fluffy white bunnies, unicorns and rainbows, and lower your blood pressure. Sleep better. Eliminate stress."

"You must be so relaxed," people tell me when they hear that I've just returned from a marathon meditation event. It takes too long to explain the truth, so I just concentrate on not choking them. Even if people have a slightly deeper understanding, a "spiritual" interpretation of meditation, it's just a different fantasy. This is the one where you are imagined clothed in white, preferably in some sort of ethnic costume that includes prayer beads, radiating a golden aura of purity, so close to holy that you may actually be levitating slightly like a magnetic German bullet train. All is bliss, tranquility, and harmony, and no one ever has to fart.

Sadhana, really treading the spiritual path, is a bitch. It requires a level of commitment to a process whose outcome seems unclear and whose path is obscure. Real transformation equals purification, dissolving identification with every small, petty, constricting and limiting thought and emotion. They all have one last party on their way out, and they leave you the bill. No slight, no matter how petty or how far in your past, is too small to dig up and obsess over when the energy hits you. And of course there's plenty to obsess about in the present.

For example, when the purification starts, nothing is good enough. Your room is too small, too dirty, too many floors up, too far down the street; the food isn't hot enough, isn't flavorful enough, is too spicy, isn't on time, isn't what you were led to believe, isn't what you want. The trip is too expensive, too inconvenient, a rip-off—you're being exploited. Your seat isn't good enough; pushy fellow seekers who beat you to your coveted spot block your view. If only you could snap your fingers and make some of them disappear—maybe all of them! Maybe you could shoot them out to space in a little capsule and get some undivided attention from your spiritual teacher, and perfect compassion will be yours.

Now I must confess to an idiosyncratic prejudice. At every meditation event I am waiting for some tangible, physical effect. I am well aware of the mental and emotional effects, but there's just something about the physical that I trust as "real." The body doesn't lie. If the teacher can blast me with energy so powerful I can physically feel it from across the room, it seems miraculous. I figure I've gotten my money's worth.

I can't explain such physical occurrences. I don't understand them, even when they are explained to me. But I am absolutely, positively certain that they happen. There are many subtle experiences that I can discount, but not the physical ones. They keep me in the game, past all reason, at great expense and considerable hassle. Having a physical experience is important to me.

In the final fifteen minutes of a five-day meditation, something physical did indeed begin to happen. A feeling of pressure was building up in the room to an unbearable crescendo. Mark was on his feet, and the Brahmins were reaching a fevered pitch. Some sort of climax was approaching, and while my attention had wandered considerably over the previous five long days, there was no chance of that happening now. I was locked on. The feeling that Something Big Was About To Happen was so strong that I assumed everyone must be feeling it. But this was not the case.

Hours earlier, Sunil, the Indian mala maker, asked me if he could sit down near my feet, just to my left. He explained that he needed the light to do his work, which was fitting silver caps onto rudraksha beads and stringing them on a wire. He was trying to finish malas for some in our group before we left town. I told him he could sit on my left. Then I went to the rooftop to look down at the fire ceremony from a different perspective, watch the sun set over the Ganges, and listen to the chanting of our Brahmins being broadcast over the city by giant cone-shaped loudspeakers.

I returned to my seat to find that Sunil had taken advantage by considerably enlarging his territory. In fact, he had done everything short of opening an internet-based business in front of me. His equipment had quadrupled and was now spread out where my feet had been for the past five days. This was annoying, but I rolled with it. I moved my seat back. I tried to focus on the ceremony.

Sunil decided that now was the time to give some previously promised instruction in his craft to a Hard Light student. I couldn't believe the audacity. Now I had a jewelry-making school in session at my feet. Sunil was apparently oblivious to the fact that it might be rude to carry on a full-blown conversation during the final minutes of a religious ceremony—his religion, mind you—in a temple, on the holiest day of the year in the Hindu calendar. I was seething. But that wasn't the worst thing.

As the fire ceremony reached its climax, the pressure of meditative energy in the room was so intense that I felt like my whole body was being squeezed. Then something extraordinary happened, the very thing I was waiting for. Some kind of force, a swirling vibration of energy, began downloading directly into the top of my head. There was no dismissing it: I was an empty vessel, and a gentle whirlpool, warm and buzzy, was filling me up with something wonderful.

It was at this exact minute that Sunil finished one of his malas, proudly delivered it to his customer, and proceeded to open a discussion of its merits right in front of me. It was of course also right in front of Mark, and seven chanting Brahmins. At the very holiest, most miraculous of moments, one that I had traveled 10,000 miles and sat countless hours to experience, I found myself simultaneously reveling in awe, and wanting to kill my fellow man. Now *that's* sadhana.

You may think I've been too hard on Varanasi. I will admit that over the course of a week there, the place gradually began to grow on me. I came to admire the idea of making as much noise as you want, day or night, in the service of religious fervor. I noticed that I needed less and less energy to repel the touts. I experienced unexpected moments of startling beauty.

I watched a group of people worshiping the river Ganges as a goddess and waving lights to Her at dusk. A baby monkey took offered grapes directly from my hand and stuffed his cheeks full, wide-eyed at his good fortune. When I was alone in the temple and sitting very still, a mongoose appeared from the rafters and ran all over the hall in curiosity, carefully examining and tasting our ceremonial preparations. I heard mind-blowing displays of musical virtuosity in concerts of traditional Indian music.

And one night I saw a boat on the Ganges release a hundred candles floating on leaves, one after another. As they floated downstream they spread out gently over a huge area, forming a glowing necklace on the black neck of the holy river.

I ended my stay in Varanasi with a lengthy, comprehensive tour of some of the numberless temples in the city. The sun was hot, and as I started to heat stroke, all of the commentary began to swirl together into one big myth. "Vishnu was carrying his wife and dropped her earring here, and that's why this spring exists and the water is holy. This is where Paul Bunyan dragged his ax, forming a river. Brahman, in his infinite glory, gave birth to Vishnu, who out of perfect love formed Shiva and his consort Parvati..."

I couldn't take any more. I spoke up.

"Then Shiva turned to his beloved Parvati and uttered the first words ever spoken in the universe: 'You want boat?'"

Dream Following Shivaratri

Christinea Johnson

February 22, 2001

Swooshing at the speed of light,
thousands of scenes whooshing by...mayhem,
births, weddings, funerals, murder,
sex, lunch...the stampede of appearances
throughout space and time......
......luminous neutrality.

The Cosmic Cave

Eva Stattine

From the moment we arrived in India we entered a stream in which time and space were virtual realities. It seemed as though one continuous, unbroken moment swept us from the very beginning to the very end of our trip. India vibrates with such intensity that a traveler there is either shaken up and turned upside down or simply yields and ends up slipping in between the seconds into the formless and timeless where India takes *you (the traveler)* on a journey.

Though it is nearly impossible to extract just one experience out of our ecstatic journey, I think one of the most outrageous times I had while traveling with Mark was a visit to the "Cosmic Cave" near Ellora. The "Cosmic Cave" is the cave where Meher Baba spent a good amount of time in meditation, and where, according to him, Shirdi Sai Baba attained enlightenment. We stayed at a guesthouse a few hundred yards from this cosmic hilltop cave. The cave could hold about eight people including Mark. On this particular evening Mark intended to meditate through the night with the sangha members taking shifts, going into the cave and meditating with him for an hour or so and then coming out and meditating in various places around the cave.

The evening began with a hike up to the cave at dusk. The path to the top of the hill took us past a number of scattered ancient mosques and tombs, weathered and half standing from centuries of monsoon seasons. Mark was already there, and the first group went in to sit with him. Not far from the cave's entrance I made a seat where I would meditate for the night. I could see the distant lights of Ellora as the last bit of dusk faded into darkness.

On the horizon there were clouds that appeared to be rapidly floating towards us on a strong warm breeze. The wind encircled my body as I watched the clouds, now lighting up with electricity, coming closer and closer to the hilltop. Over the course of maybe an hour the soft gray clouds spread to cover more of the night sky as bursts of foggy light danced within them. It was a marvelous sight. From the moment I arrived at this sacred place and began to meditate, the energy kept rising higher and higher and becoming more and more intense. By the time the clouds had made their way to hover over the cave, I thought that at any moment the whole hilltop would detach from the rest of the land and blast off through the electrified clouds into infinity, taking us with it. Just when I thought the experience was coming to a crescendo, it was time to go in and meditate with Mark.

Crawling into the wonderfully warm, candle-lit cave was like entering the Divine Mother's womb. The energy was fantastically serene and strong. It was certainly the peak of all the peak experiences I had in India. It was unfathomably yet unmistakably inter-dimensional and the most clear, God-filled space I've ever entered. There was a part of me that never wanted to leave. Fortunately, I feel the resonance of that night with me still today. ✪

A Night on Cosmic Mountain

Barbara Jo Fleming

I pad from shade to sun and shade again, savoring the changing temperatures of the ancient cut-stone beneath my bare feet. Nine times—clockwise—twenty paces to a side, I circumambulate in Buddhist fashion the elevated walkway. At each of the four directions, I reach to caress window ledges, worn to shallow curves by countless hands seeking blessings. I bring that touch to my heart. Spiky beads of my *Shivite mala* roll through thumb and middle finger of my left hand, synchronized with sustained, measured breaths. The index finger, the finger of the ego—stands detached, not touching the beads, as dictated by energy channels that run through the body and by metaphor. Mystical mathematics pulses through my chakras: 108 beads, 108 breaths, 108 chants of *Omnamashivaya*—Sanskrit syllables rising and descending within my spine.

Crowning the domed tomb that I circle, an exotic spire pierces seven stacked globes. The globes designate the profound level of spiritual attainment of the Sufi saint entombed here. Two neighboring tombs, a hundred meters away and pinnacled with three and five globes apiece, frame the mountain peak that appears gloriously before me, each time I turn the northwest corner of the building.

A jolting sensation shoots through my toes as the arch of my foot catches the edge of an uneven paving stone. My teacher has said that the falling of my arches is a spiritual thing, that it connects me more deeply with the earth, but it's hard to fathom. In reality, I've become dependent on orthodics and rarely go barefoot because of the pain—except here in India where shoes are forbidden in the holy sites. Here, I hobble on the outside of my foot, return to my chant, and round the last corner.

Before I enter the tomb, I cover my blond head with the translucent scarf of my Punjabi: an outfit of pants under a mid-calf-length dress, concocted from Salvation Army Thrift Store purchases. My imitation of Indian women is awkward. Feigning culture I scarcely understand, I never quite get it right: Too much intention and enthusiasm for the gestures that should happen without thought. The miscreant length of turquoise silk relentlessly misbehaves, threatens to strangle me, drags through questionable substances on the ground, and escapes me entirely—exposing the taboo silhouette of my tits. Though my costume is inauthentic and I feel like a child playing dress-up, I've come to India to play another game. The silk scarf is easy compared to the game of awakening with its veil of illusion that mercilessly toys with me.

I enter the tomb, a Spartan room dominated by a massive stone crypt in the center. Around me, the energy of the entombed saint wells up...a soft cloud of stillness, slightly blissful, unexpectedly palpable. I know little of this being—neither name nor history—only the story the building tells: Sufi, revered, seventh-level *Nirvikalpa Samadhi*, and dead...a long while, judging by the weathered stones.

I bow at the foot of the rectangular crypt, seeking blessing and wondering "*Why? What's the use? What's the meaning?*" The Buddhist-trained part of my brain deliberately answers my neurotic mind, "*No use. No meaning. Everyone deserves blessing, even me. Be present. Now.*" I disengage from the litany and open myself to the Awakened One.

My forehead rests on the cool stone, made smooth by innumerable bowed heads. I wait. I restrain expectation, still hoping for a glimpse of *Samadhi*. Transmission is a gift not a given. Where my forehead contacts the crypt, a blissful current begins to stream through to the center of my skull. The glowing charge intensifies and, after a time, recedes gently. I stand, humbled by this small unveiling of the divine...mystified once again by the flagrant, unfathomable magic of India.

My fingertips trail down to brush the doorjamb as I leave the tomb. Ignoring my mind's condemnation, "*Superstition,*" I cherish the ritual that I do not fully understand. Outside, I find my sandals. Grateful that for one more day, no one has walked away with them, I wiggle into the flip-flops, purchased for their indistinctive appearance that belies the expensive arch support that they provide.

Next to the lichen-encrusted wall, I gather my too-many belongings. They overflow from my expanding net bag, embarrassingly *unsadhu*-like: water bottle, headlamp, self-inflating REI pillow, fleece jacket, folding camp stool, bed pillow from the guest house, handmade pads for my ankles, meditation shawl, protein bar—most items carried half-way around the world. I chuckle disparagingly at the lengths I go to avoid the threat of discomfort during the coming eight-hour meditation on the mountain.

The lengthening shadows of the three Mosques' spires extend knobby fingers far beyond the enclosed courtyard, toward the slope. The saintly trio, sentinels of the mountain trail, direct me unmistakably through the high arching stone gate toward my destination—the Cosmic Cave. The cliché alliteration brings to mind psychedelic pseudo-seekers of the '60s, but the cosmic history of the cave supersedes that image. Spiritual masters, avatars, and great sages have through the ages used the cave as a base camp for universal work—doing whatever it is that these mysterious beings do. No doubt the three guys interred in these tombs walked up the same path and meditated in the cave as well, before their discarded bodies became anchors to the mountain's energy vortex.

I follow the snaking path that is littered with quartz crystals edged in the brilliant green of oxidized copper. Clutching my unwieldy bundle of attachment and aversion, I slip and struggle up the increasingly steep trail. Below and above, I see others in small groups converging on the cave with similar bundles of their own.

Twenty minutes later, I reach the cave nestled just below the summit. Subdued sangha members set up their meditation digs. Murmuring voices relay the order of the evening. The first eight meditators are already inside the cave. We will do shifts of an hour-and-a-half within the cave. Carefully, I settle onto my three-legged folding stool made more unstable than usual by the uneven ground.

Spread out before me, a spectacular quilt of sprawling farmland draws my gaze. Prayers rising from the local Mosques as the sun touches the horizon seem to rally clouds on the mountains across the rural valley. The pastel clouds poof into existence and change hues with the sunset.

The wind suddenly picks up, and I grab my red meditation shawl to prevent it from flying away with the bats that streak across the dusty orange sky and the littered plastic bags that swirl wildly in the gusts. The sangha members, wrapped in bright shawls lashed out in the wind, look like Tibetan prayer flags strung across the mountain face to stragglers still approaching. One small group zigzags up the slope with flashlights flitting erratically. Another group near the bottom with a single steady beam, strikes directly up the incline towards us, ignoring the switchback trail altogether.

Lightning raggedly dissects the darkening sky. Three-second delayed booms counterpoint the snapping shawls. The air smells of burnt metal, electrically charged, more exhilarating than a mere storm. Banks of magnetism, dropping pressure, raw power, and a sense of curious intelligence sweep across the mountain. Elementals gather, drawn by the commotion in and around the cave, stirred by the forces being tapped. Definitely not your everyday weather front.

The crystal and copper mountain, an antennae and amplifier for spiritual work, pours out a gale of energy. Meditation overtakes me, rather than my engaging it. A heavily amped internal space surges, vamps, and shakes loose an avalanche of thoughts, too dense to think. I can only let go and tumble with it.

Voices and a bustle of activity draw me halfway out of meditation. The beeline group with the single light has arrived. The men cue single-file through the twenty of us meditators perched unmoving alongside the trail. They stop and converse a long while with the local caretaker of the holy site, who sits outside the cave entrance.

Buffeted by the wind, non-English male voices fade in and out of hearing. The locals surround the caretaker and the boxes of flowers at his feet. It seems he answers at least some of their questions satisfactorily for they leave again and take a meandering path through us, certainly puzzling over the mix of Western luxury and *saddhu* intensity of our meditation style. Their melodic voices trail off into the distance, and I sink heavily into the meditation.

An hour later, the first group of meditators emerges from the cave and files past to find their places in the dark. Someone touches my arm and whispers that I should go in. I head towards the entrance half dazed. From the caretaker, a compact man in his thirties, I receive a handful of flowers. I feel a surge of gratitude that this offering has been prepared for me. His smile is bright and sweet as he encourages me to enter. I set the roses on the hip-high threshold, grip the open white metal grating to hoist myself up, and clamber into the rough opening.

The energy inside the cave is as staggeringly still as the outside energy is torrential—the contrast startling. Mark sits against the whitewashed side wall, his bulky form huge in the low ceiling space. An altar with photos of Meher Baba, Muktananda, and other saints spreads across the far end of the shallow cave, perhaps eight feet from the entrance. Red roses and marigolds adorn the altar, lavishly strung by the caretaker in preparation for our visit. I place my flowers on the altar and prostrate myself for a few moments on the canvas floor covering, my body in full contact with the cave surface. I touch the feet of my teacher, affirm my intention to surrender the illusion that separates me from the divine, and send off a prayer for open, light-heartedness—and, as always, for awakening.

I find a place, my back propped against the uneven stone. Others file in behind me and perform their own version of the ritual, which varies widely depending on how much of the Oriental trappings they can comfortably integrate. Some do nothing more than a slight bow. The nine of us with folded legs, knees touching, occupy the entire space not designated as altar. On my compact, high-tech cushion, I ready myself for an ancient, wild ride. Mark gives brief meditation instructions, his voice already characteristically hoarse from the energy coursing through him. We meditate.

The night passes timelessly; meditators file in and out of the Cosmic Cave; some retreat down the mountain towards the guesthouse. The same group of chatty locals wanders through a couple more times, and a few raindrops fall—not enough to get us wet but enough to bless us. At times, I sit on the ground, my back flush against the prodding rocks of the cave's exterior. Staying alert is surprisingly easy in this energy, though twice, I barely catch my teetering stool as I pitch toward the cliff.

Finally, my field seems so saturated, nerve endings so raw that further meditation seems impossible. I focus on my breath, watch the lightning across the valley, and relish the wind that blusters about while we sit under stars.

At about two in the morning, the last group emerges from the cave and heads down the mountain. A few of us linger to walk down with Mark. He crawls to the cave entrance and with help, he sits. His uncooperative body fills the cave opening; his legs dangle from the ledge. The night is calm. The storm, lightning, and wind stopped when the meditation ended, as concisely as they began with it. Mark tells us in a raspy whisper that often during deep states of *Samadhi*, the over-stimulated nervous system becomes unresponsive. He cannot stand nor walk. His nervous system will come back online in a few hours; he reassures us and crawls back into the cave to wait for the dawn when the trail will be less treacherous. At his request, two men accompany him back into the cave

Quenched, exhilarated, and reluctant to have the night end, the rest of us pick our way slowly along the trail in the bobbing flashlight pools. I think that I am managing my array of possessions much better on the way down, and in the next moment, I find myself sliding on my ass down a particularly gravely patch of trail. I sit for a couple of breaths still holding my bundle that somehow has stayed contained on my lap. The silence of the night wraps velvety around me. An ironic peace wells up, disregarding my clumsiness, my bruised bottom, and my ongoing chagrin once again triggered by my…oh-so-much stuff. The playful pretense I had entertained en route to the cave has been supplanted by a deep, abiding sense of authenticity. The veil has subtly shifted. Immense quiet expands within me, and later in the early hours before dawn, permeates my dreams. ✿

The Garland

Linda Horan

The Hard Light Sangha arrived in Meherabad on March 1st 2005. Our visit was to be short—one night only. Most of our group was assigned space in one of several dormitories. Two women, Pat and I, were accommodated in the main lodge, Pilgrim House.

There were eight beds in our room. I'm not sure if every bed was filled but, besides Pat and me, there were at least four other women in the room that night. My bed was on an aisle next to the door; I was appreciative of the extra space and extra breeze that this particular slot afforded.

I do not remember the name of the woman whose bed was to my left. She was very striking, tall and lean with chiseled features and an accent that I couldn't place. I tried to pinpoint its origin—Belgium, England, South Africa perhaps. She was dressed completely in black and wore a turban. She looked and moved like a ballerina.

As we shared introductions, the woman told me that she and her boyfriend were traveling around the world and their journey brought them to Meherabad. I recall that at that point she had been staying at Baba's ashram for several weeks. Before the lights went out for the night, my enchanting roommate told me that a great time to visit the *samadhi*, the tomb where Baba is buried, was before the shrine opened, during the hour it is cleaned. I asked if anyone could assist in the cleaning. She encouraged me to come early and find out.

The next morning I awoke around 5:00 a.m.; only a handful of others in Pilgrim House were also starting their day. I washed and dressed and made my way to the samadhi shrine. By the time I arrived around 5:45 there was already a line of 10 to 15 people waiting for the shrine to open. Several others were inside the samadhi, apparently performing the morning rituals of which my friend had spoken. It seemed that I was too late for an opportunity to assist with cleaning, so I took my place in the *darshan* line.

The person coordinating the activity within the samadhi was an Indian woman. She would bring items into the shrine, then return outside and keep an eye on the growing line of devotees. At one point, she scanned the queue and approached several people, including me, and handed us garlands. I assumed that as we went through the darshan line, we would place these first flowers of the day on Baba's tomb. I was intensely moved that I'd been blessed with this honor.

I stood in line, reverently holding the garland while trying to establish my highest alignment, my deepest presence. After a brief wait, the samadhi was apparently ready to be opened. The Indian woman signaled to me and the three other flower bearers and beckoned us to approach.

She told us to enter the shrine and stand on Baba's tomb. Each of us took a space on the lower half of the marble slab, mine in the left hand corner nearest the door. As the four of us stood there I struggled to maintain my awareness, my attention. I was standing on the bones of the Avatar, the Original Soul. I was electrified, shocked.

The Indian woman pointed to me and indicated that I should put my garland on the tomb. Put my garland on the tomb . . . where? Put it WHERE? There was nothing else on the tomb. The area that our positions described was at least five to six feet long and over four feet wide. Do I put the garland at the top of that expanse? In the middle? Do I place the garland so that it is in an oval shape? A heart shape? Straight?

An image flashed through my mind. I couldn't quite capture it; it was more of a feeling than a visual. I got down on my hands and knees and crawled on the tomb, toward the middle, near the bottom edge. I was operating on blind instinct. Tantric shadows were casting flickering impressions from the depths of my psyche. I felt the stencil of a sacred syllable, resting on a lotus, dissolving into a moon disc. I took my garland and placed it at the bottom of the tomb and tried to find the shape that was the appropriate foundation of all the other garlands that would be heaped on Baba's tomb that day. I would have arranged the blossoms for as long as it took to express the perfect gesture, but I felt that the time allotted for such fussing had ended. I crawled back to my corner and stood up.

The placement of my garland was more suggestive of a moustache than a moon disc. How could I have not seen? It was now so terribly obvious that I should have laid the garland like a wreath in the very center of the rectangle, providing a perfect base for the next garland, and the next, and the next. The Indian woman knows I am a fool.

The other flower bearers offer their garlands. How were theirs positioned in relation to mine? I don't know. Somehow I got out of the samadhi shrine. I don't know how. I had ruined everything. For the rest of this incarnation I would have to live with the fact that I did not properly position the first garland on the grave of the Avatar. I was faint with regret.

I sat outside of Baba's Room for a while in stunned paralysis. There was no going back, there was no second chance. I don't know how long I remained there, but I couldn't move until I digested the reality that there was nothing more I could do. It was over. I walked back to the Pilgrim House and got on with the rest of my life.

Later that day, before the Hard Light group left Meherabad, I wandered back to Baba's samadhi shrine. I took my place in line with the others waiting for darshan. As I approached the door of the samadhi and entered, I could barely stand to look. With trepidation, I raised my eyes. A mountain of flowers on Baba's tomb covered the entire expanse the four of us defined earlier that morning. The mound of garlands did not seem to have been impacted by its distorted foundation. I made my prayers and took my leave.

* * *

Several months later, I was preparing Hard Light's kitchen for the Gurushakti Summer Retreat in Taos. As chief cook on many retreats, one of my most important rituals is the creation of the kitchen altar, the *puja*. Through all the years, the assembly of a puja remains a wildly mystical process. I don't build the kitchen puja; the puja manifests of it own accord like a dream out of the very fabric of retreat.

I felt the puja coming into being. I remembered a digital photograph of Meher Baba's samadhi that someone had given to me a year or so earlier at my request. I searched my hard drive and located the file. As the photograph flashed open on screen, my life that had ended that day in Meherabad was resurrected. The placement of the single garland on Baba's tomb bore a semblance to the placement of "my" garland. This photo became the crown jewel around which the kitchen altar revolved.

The Gurushakti Retreat produced an inconceivable field of revelation. The unity, the interdependence—of God, of Guru, and of Self—was unavoidable. The photo of Meher Baba's samadhi from the retreat kitchen now resides on my altar at home. It is not a mere photograph. Like all the other images on my puja, it is a reflection of an eternal portal that the image depicts. I will always be crawling on the Bones of the Avatar. ✲

Hard Light Commandos smuggle Guru out of India
Mark Bonnlander

Leap of Faith

Fernando Escobar

It is 4:32 p.m. I'm flying on a plane and we are almost home, although I feel like I just left home. I left my family, my country, my friends for teachers, bells, drums, and chants. Recalling what we just went through, I'm still amazed it happened. What did happen? Why so much grace and fortune? I feel extremely fortunate and lucky: such is the love from Nityananda, Meher Baba, Shri Sai Baba, etc. Well, as a friend of mine says, "Go with it!" I'll run with it like it's the Olympic torch. So much to recall: Ganeshpuri, the Yatra, and Rishikesh, and participating in bathing a statue of Nityananda with milk. Baba Muktananda was right in saying that a guru the caliber of Bhagavan Nityananda is rare.

I'll never forget that Yagna (fire ceremony) though. Being a part of it was an honor. And my story is about a friend I met there that showed me how to do *it*, the way to offer this body to God, Guru, and Self. My friend was a spider.

I'll never forget that beautiful spider. As I "Swaha-d" black sesame seeds into the fire, he came around the corner and stood still. Did he acknowledge me or something? I admired the form of the jagged yellow lines on his legs surrounding the darkness of his body. "What are you doing here?" I thought, "You are going to get burned, so be careful." He jumps onto the first level of the pit: Physical body. "Swaha," I say. He meditates on his decision as I look around to see if anyone else sees the spider; everyone is *within* or somewhere else. He jumps to the second level: Subtle body. "Swaha?" I repeat, worried he doesn't know where he's going but it seems like he's actually thinking. He jumps to the third level of the pit: Causal body. "Swaha?!" as I put in more sesame seeds. I witness the spider building up courage, but for what? "Swaha!!!" He jumps into the fire: Atman! He was contemplating his last moment before abandoning everything for the grace of the fire! My God! The spider jumped into the pit right in front of me. I never knew an insect could do such a thing, with purpose, and cause such a mark on my life. "So that's how it's done!" I thanked him.

Let's do it. May this plane in this endless blue sky fly straight into the bright orange Sun. I want to do it now just like my friend the spider! Ready and going all the way. Wait a minute! The clouds underneath begin to creep up; dark and hazy clouds. Underneath is the filthy smog of confusion, paranoia, forgetfulness, and loneliness. Lights come from the ground and it looks like a city of lost angels. The plane descends but why? I was going to the Sun, to God. I'm ready for the *leap of faith*! This situation is familiar in long journeys. But I guess there is no need to worry. It's just another layover. ✺

It's Time to Go Back

Pat Cookinham

India called yesterday…and then again today.

Yesterday my hall was Delhi Airport with its own peculiar odor.
Men with guns stood guard, not your holstered hidden pistols
but long rifles that say "I mean business."
Traders ply esoteric Eastern wares
beside a franchised sandwich shop and trinket store—
the only place in India that sells refrigerator magnets
(or so it seems).
Leaving the terminal…a smoky smell.
Beings support me on every side, sometimes too closely.
Hands grabbing and mouths pleading for alms.
Children stealing because they're hungry.
Picture this against a backdrop of skyscrapers
that speak of wealth and opulence,
This is Delhi.

Then today, Ganeshpuri trickled in while I was at my computer,
a lighter scent but still India.
I drift silently on the flow of Ganeshpuri
feeling the veil that separates the many worlds,
sensing the nearness of our Gurus.

I'm sitting there, in Murli's shop,
drinking coffee. A fine blend his neighbor buys.
It's the coffee that's India—half hot cream with sugar.
I never drink it that way at home.
They offer me a chair; bring the cloths for me to see.
I buy because the cloths are brightly colored,
and, besides, it seems the thing to do.

I miss the mad dash to have an outfit made

or clothes ironed for a party.
I long to meander through the square, giving the cows a bite to eat.
I now hear only the echoes of bells and chants that call to service—
that's not enough.
Mostly, I want to be with Mark,
just sitting in the upstairs balcony, not doing, just sitting.

This is Ganeshpuri.

It's time to go back.

Glossary

Avatar: The descent of God or simply an incarnation of God.

Awakening: Realization of one's union with God.

Bellows Breath: Pranayama meditation breath technique.

Brahmin: Hindu of the highest caste traditionally assigned to the priesthood.

Burning Man: Annual art festival and temporary community based on radical self-expression and self-reliance in the Black Rock Desert of Nevada.

Chakra: (*lit.* wheel): Any of the primary energy centers in the body suspended within sushumna. Psychic centers that illuminate and activate the brain. The primary chakras are Muladhara (root chakra), Svadhisthana (genital chakra), Manipura (navel chakra), Anahata (heart chakra), Vishudha (throat chakra), Ajna (forehead chakra), and Sahasrar (crown chakra).

Chela: The disciple or student of a Guru or sage.

Darshan: Seeing or being in the presence of a revered person, sacred image, or sacred place.

Dharma: The Way; the study of truth.

Enlightenment: Stabilization of God consciousness in the physical body. The total purification of obscurations and ignorance, and the total expansion of wisdom to all levels of being.

Four Bodies: The four aspects of the human form: the physical (material) body, the subtle (energetic) body, the causal (mental) body and the super-causal body (Atman).

Ganeshpuri: Indian village north of Mumbai; seat of the Siddha lineage and home of the Nityananda temple. The bones of both Nityananda and Muktananda rest in Ganeshpuri.

Ganges River (*or*: Ganga): Sacred river that is life, purity, and a goddess to the people of India. Anyone who touches the purifying waters of "Mother Ganges" is said to be cleansed of all sins.

Ghat: A broad flight of steps situated on an Indian riverbank that provides access to the water, especially for bathing. The Raja Ghat is located on the banks of the Ganges in Varanasi, India.

Grace: Gift from God.

Grace of the Guru: The means by which one can be liberated and circumvent the full process of the laws of karma.

Guru: The word Guru is comprised of gu (darkness), the formless hidden power of God, and ru (illumination), the beauty and luster of living beings. Teacher or Guide to spiritual illumination.

Hard Light (*or:* Hard Light Center of Awakening): Center of spiritual study in Los Angeles founded and led by Mark Griffin. Griffin uses a mystical approach to meditation, accenting direct experience and personal practice in the search for enlightenment.

Ida and Pingala: The two main nadis located in the spinal column of the subtle body, on either side of the sushumna. The ida, known as the moon nadi, is located on the left side and is red in color. The pingala, referred to as the sun nadi, is located on the right side and is white in color.

Karma: Law of cause and effect. Physical, verbal or mental action that shapes one's destiny.

Kumba Mela: Great roving spiritual festival that has moved among four sites in India for more than four thousand years. Millions of the Hindu faithful gather to wash away their sins in the holy waters of the Ganges.

Kundalini (*lit.* coiled one): Dormant spiritual energy held at the base of the spine and awakened by shaktipat initiation.

The Ladder: Art creation by Mark Griffin, founder and teacher of Hard Light. This 108 foot ladder was raised to become free-standing in the desert of Nevada at the 2005 Burning Man gathering.

Lakshmi (or: Laxmi): Goddess of prosperity and wealth; consort of Vishnu.

Liberation: Freedom from the cycle of birth and death. State of realization of oneness with the Absolute.

Lineage: The link of guru to guru to disciple and God; pathway of transmission of grace.

Mahasamadhi: This, according to Hindu tradition, is an enlightened master's conscious exit from the body at the time of his physical death.

Mala: A string of beads for keeping count of the mantra or prayers one is saying.

Mantra: Sacred words or sounds invested with the power to transform and protect the one who repeats them; God in the form of sound. Mantras are the condensed essence of the reality from which they spring.

Meditation: Any of a number of practices that focus, hone, or quiet the mind.

Meditation Intensive: The Intensive is a full day program designed to expose participants, through a series of meditations, to the powerful energies of samadhi, kundalini, and shaktipat.

Meditation Retreat: Retreats at Hard Light are concentrated three- to five-day sessions held in remote locations in which one can more fully immerse one's self in the internal practices without the distractions of daily life.

Meher Baba: Most recent incarnation of the Original Soul; Avatar. God in human form. His bones are enshrined in Meherabad, India.

Nadi: Pranic channel.

Nine Openings: The nine openings in the body: eyes, ears, nose, mouth, anus, and sexual organs.

Nirvikalpa Samadhi: Nir (without) and vikalpa (form or conceptualization). The highest state of samadhi, beyond all thought, attribute, and description.

Om Na Ma Shi Va Ya: Sacred chant to Lord Shiva.

Om Swa Ha: The vibration of the three psychic nerves.

Path of the Rising Sun: Following a spiritual path that looks toward the optimistic, towards the rising sun.

Prana: Breath; vital energy; life force. There are five forms of prana: *prana*, the descending life force; *apana*, the ascending life force; *samana*, the mental and cyclical life force; *viyana*, the expansion and infusion of life force; and *udhana*, the compression of life force.

Pranayama: Breath control.

Puja: An altar; ritual worship performed at an altar.

Sadhana: Spiritual practice. Sincere spiritual endeavor. Spiritual journey.

Sadhu: A monk or ascetic.

Sahasrara: The crown chakra.

Samadhi: Sama (intuitive knowledge) and dhi (the highest truth). Union with God. Bliss or absorption in God.

Samsara (*or:* Wheel of Samsara): Objective world. The eternal cycle of birth, suffering, death and rebirth.

Sangha: Conventionally, the community of spiritual aspirants. Ultimately, the sangha are those who experience ultimate reality or emptiness. These are the High Ones.

Satguru: The true Guru; a perfect Master.

Satsang: Translated from Sanskrit, satsang means "in communion with truth." It is a conversation with the Guru in which the participants communicate on many levels about the nature of Self.

The Self: Divine Consciousness, essential nature, supreme identity.

Seva: Any selfless act of service. Also, service to the Guru to promote the dharma.

Shakti: Divine energy.

Shaktipat: Descent of grace that awakens the kundalini.

Shiva: A name for the all-pervasive supreme Reality; one of the Hindu trinity of gods who represents God as the destroyer.

Shivaratri (*lit.* night of Shiva): Festival of Lord Shiva celebrated throughout India in February or March (date varies).

Siddha: Perfect one; one who has attained the state of unity awareness and experiences himself as all-pervasive; one who has achieved mastery over his senses and their objects.

So'ham (*lit.* I am That): The natural vibration of the Self which occurs spontaneously with each incoming and outgoing breath. By becoming aware of it, a yogi experiences the identity between his individual self and the supreme Self.

Subtle Body: The energetic body of a human being.

Sushumna: Primary nerve running from the base of the spine to the crown of the head; the possessor of all worlds, qualities and universes.

Three rivers: Ida, Pingala and Sushumna; the three main energy channels in the subtle body.

Universal Consciousness: Paramatman, Supreme Consciousness.

Varanasi (*or:* Kashi, Benares): Holy city sacred to Shiva located in northern India on the banks of the Ganges River. According to Hindu tradition, whoever dies in this city attains liberation.

Yagna: Spiritual ceremony performed by Hindu priests to eliminate karmic difficulties. The priest makes offerings or blessings to the Gods on behalf of the person(s) requesting the ritual.

Yatra: Spiritual journey; sacred journey.

Yoga (*lit.* union): Path and method of unification. The state of oneness with the Self; the practices leading to that state.

About Mark Griffin

Mark Griffin was born in Tacoma, Washington in 1954. His father's engineering jobs kept their family moving, and Mark grew up in West Virginia, Alabama, Illinois, and Washington.

The dawning of adolescence awakened an intuitive spiritual yearning for Enlightenment that led Mark to reach out to clergy in his community and those otherwise trained in theology. He began to research methods of cultivating the Divine, and developed a strong inner life of contemplation and prayer.

At age 17 Mark began studying art and music in San Francisco. In 1976 at age 21 Mark met Swami Muktananda, immediately recognized him as his guru, and began aggressively training in meditation. Constant contact with the transformational power of his guru repeatedly pushed Mark to his mental, emotional and physical limits. The process of purification he endured was so intense that at times it seemed life-threatening.

After six years of non-stop training Mark had just begun to enter into a rare, advanced state of universal consciousness known as samadhi when his beloved guru Muktananda died. Great Tibetan teachers of the Kagyu tradition came to his aid, and Mark received continuing instruction in maturing and stabilizing his meditation from Kalu Rinpoche and Chogyam Trungpa. Under their care he entered into nirvikalpa samadhi and became Awakened.

Mark started teaching in 1985. In 1989 he moved to Los Angeles and started the Hard Light Center of Awakening, a school of meditation dedicated to the art and science of awareness of the Self. Mark continues to create art professionally.

www.ingramcontent.com/pod-product-compliance
Lightning Source LLC
Chambersburg PA
CBHW031247290426
44109CB00012B/475